"*TeenVestor* serves as a great introduction to investing and the fundamentals of financial markets for teens… One of the greatest aspects of *TeenVestor* is that Modu has written the book in a tone that teens can relate to. He has taken a wide array of financial concepts and presented them in such a way that today's teen can easily appreciate. Modu uses examples that are simple to understand and gives practical advice that any "Teenvestor" can start applying right away."
— **Jack E. Kosakowski, President & CEO, Junior Achievement USA**

"As both the CEO of Investopedia and the father of a teenage son, I thoroughly recommend this book to both teenagers and their parents. The state of financial education in the U.S. is woeful. Schools are failing and it is up to our teenagers and parents to enable their kids to become Teenvestors. The authors' use of worksheets, real-life examples and easy-to-use format help readers gain more knowledge than after their first finance class in college, but in a much easier learning format. Concepts such as diversification, compounding, EPS and socially responsible investing were particularly well done, as well as advice for parents on managing money and teenage investing. Despite having an MBA in Finance from Wharton, I was able to gleam more than a few take-aways. As both an investor and the parent of investors, it is a must read."
— **David Siegel, CEO, Investopedia**

"Written especially for teenagers, although it's actually a good basic resource for any age… Good, solid (not dumbed down) explanations of investment basics. I like this book because it encourages parents to come along for the ride and learn about investing, too."

— **Money**

"Teens and first-time investors, this is your moment! No one is going to care more about your financial future than you, and because you have time on your side, you are in the best position to make the most of that future. Thanks to a whole host of new, affordable and easy-to-understand online investing options, there has never been a better time for the 'little guy' to take charge of his/her investments. Mr. Modu's book offers clear, concise and actionable information to help get you on the right path."
— **Donato "Don" Montanaro, Jr., CEO, TradeKing Group, Inc.**

"In-depth and sophisticated… [*TeenVestor*] doesn't assume its readers have had prior exposure to investing or easy access to money… Teens and parents will appreciate the detailed treatment of investing strategies."

— Morningstar

"When it comes to saving and budgeting, these are habits that are necessary to develop at an early age as they are crucial to creating a healthy financial future. As a teen, your ability to start saving money now, no matter what amount, will help pave the way for future stability and allow your money to grow faster through compound interest. *TeenVestor* is an excellent book that will set you on the path to being a prudent saver and a wise investor."

— Luvleen Sidhu, Co-Founder and Chief Strategy & Marketing Officer, BankMobile

"*TeenVestor* is another excellent resource for learning not only the basics of investing in stocks, mutual funds, and IRAs, but also the workings of the economy."

— Barron's

"Psst. Find this website on the internet and bookmark it. *TeenVestor.com*. Just don't let anyone know you're using it. It's supposed to be for kids. If you want to learn about investing, this is the place to go. It's for teens, but if you won't tell, we won't either. This is good stuff."

— Independent Tribune

"The authors explain the basics of investing… how to understand the stock market, and how to evaluate and choose stocks for the long-term…Accurate, objective, and helpful."

— School Library Journal

TeenVestor®

The Practical Investment Guide for Teens and Their Parents

Emmanuel Modu
Nkem Modu
Andrea Walker-Modu

A TeenBusiness Media Publication

Published by TeenBusiness Media
P.O. Box 1968
Livingston, New Jersey 07039

This publication is designed to provide accurate and authoritative information with regard to the subject matter covered. It is sold with the understanding that the publisher is not engaged in rendering legal, accounting, or other professional advice. If legal advice or other expert assistance is required, the services of a qualified professional person should be sought. — *From a Declaration of Principles jointly adopted by a Committee of the American Bar Association and a Committee of Publishers and Associations.*

Publisher's Cataloging-in-Publication Data

Modu, Emmanuel, author.
    [Teenvestor.com]
    Teenvestor: the practical investment guide for teens
and their parents / Emmanuel Modu, Nkem Modu, and Andrea
Walker-Modu. -- First TeenBusiness Media edition.
    pages cm
    Includes index.
    Original edition published as: Teenvestor.com.
Newark, N.J. : Gateway Publishers, 2000. Previous
edition published as: Teenvestor. New York : Berkley
Publishing Group, ©2002.
    ISBN 978-0-9974892-0-0

    1. Teenagers--Finance, Personal. 2. Investments.
3. Finance, Personal.   I. Modu, Nkem, author.
II. Walker-Modu, Andrea, author. III. Title.

HG179.M566 2017   332.60835
                   QBI16-600057

Acknowledgements

In *TeenVestor®: The Practical Investment Guide for Teens and Their Parents*, we seek to demystify an activity that although as old as time itself, has been thought to be the domain of a select and always, older crowd. However, we are delighted with the dramatic increase in Teenvesting since the book's first publication. Admittedly, there have been significant changes in the world of investing. New tools, platforms, technologies, all of which are described in the following pages are available, and yes, even tailored to a much younger generation.

We have substantially revised *TeenVestor*, to continue our mission of explaining the world of investing and encouraging responsible investing by teens. This important goal could not have been achieved without the tremendous support, encouragement and advice from our family. *TeenVestor's* journey has been, and continues to be our labor of love.

We dedicate this book in loving memory of our own Dr. C. C. Modu. Papa, we hope you enjoy this read from wherever you are.

Emmanuel, Andrea and Nkem

About TeenBusiness Media

TeenBusiness Media is the publisher of *TeenVestor®: The Practical Investment Guide for Teens and Their Parents*. TeenBusiness Media is the provider of information of interest to teens related to investing, entrepreneurship, economics, employment, and other activities that will prepare them for a productive and well-rounded life. Among the websites operated by TeenBusiness Media are TeenVestor.com and TeenBusiness.com. The company also manages the following twitter accounts: @teenvestor, @teenmogul, @girlceos, and @kindteens.

TeenVestor®: The Practical Investment Guide for Teens and Their Parents is available at special discounts for bulk purchases for sales promotions, premiums, fund-raising, or educational use. For details please send an email to: contact@teenbusiness.com. Interested parties can also write to: TeenBusiness Media, P.O. Box 1968, Livingston, New Jersey 07039.

About the Authors

Emmanuel Modu is currently a Managing Director at a major rating agency, a former vice president at Citibank and J.P. Morgan Chase, and a former senior treasury analyst at Merrill Lynch. He is the author of *The Lemonade Stand: A Guide to Encouraging The Entrepreneur In Your Child* and co-author of *Mad Cash: A First Timer's Guide to Investing $30 to $3,000*. Emmanuel holds an MBA from the University of Pennsylvania's Wharton School and an electrical engineering degree from Princeton University.

Nkem Modu is the Lead IOS Developer at an online streaming company. Nkem is also the Chief Content Director for TeenBusiness Media properties including: TeenBusiness.com; TeenVestor.com; and the twitter handles, @teenvestor, @teenmogul, @girlceos, and @kindteens. He attended The Taft School and Trinity College.

Andrea Walker-Modu is currently a Senior Vice President at a global banking institution, and was an attorney for the Federal Reserve Bank of New York and for Paul, Weiss, Rifkind, Wharton & Garrison. She is the co-author of *Mad Cash: A First Timer's Guide to Investing $30 to $3,000*. Andrea attended Princeton University, is also a graduate of The George Washington University Law School and Seton Hall Law School, where she received her Master of Laws.

TABLE OF CONTENTS

FOREWORD

It is never too early to begin to understand how investing works. Unfortunately, too many Americans don't take on the responsibility of informed investing until they are years into their work life. The result has been under-funded 401K plans, insufficient "rainy day" funds for emergencies, and a general lack of financial preparedness for retirement and the challenges that may occur in day-to-day life.

Emmanuel Modu's *TeenVestor* serves as a great introduction to investing and the fundamentals of financial markets for teens. The way our markets work can be intimidating, even for financially savvy adults. Modu's book simplifies concepts that might appear abstract at first, but helps teens, and their parents, gain a better understanding of how debt and equity markets work...and how they can work for you as an investor.

One of the greatest aspects of *TeenVestor* is that Modu has written the book in a tone that teens can relate to. He has taken a wide array of financial concepts and presented them in such a way that today's teen can easily appreciate. Modu uses examples that are simple to understand and gives practical advice that any "teenvestor" can start applying right away.

For parents, this book creates a great opportunity to help their children acquire the tools they need to be empowered to make financially responsible decisions. From paying for college to making the decision to make a 401K contribution in that first job, young adults are faced with many financial decisions that will follow them throughout their lives. *TeenVestor* can help you and your child get a head start on those decisions and plot a course for a financially successful future.

Financial literacy is a major focus for Junior Achievement. Each year, millions of young people, with the help of hundreds of thousands of volunteers, learn critical financial concepts. Books such as *TeenVestor* are additional essential tools that help our young people become more financially literate and responsible.

TeenVestor is a book every teen, and their parents, should read. It takes a concept that can be intimidating for many, the need to own your financial future, and puts it in terms that are understandable and actionable. It only takes a few hours to read, but contains lessons that will last a lifetime.

Jack E. Kosakowski
President & CEO
Junior Achievement USA

INTRODUCTION I
(for Teenvestors)

You are holding in your hands the first investment book written especially for teenagers and their parents. In addition, the book's companion website, www.teenvestor.com, is full of information to make you a smarter and more prudent investor.

Once you start learning how to invest, you will be transformed from a teenager to a Teenvestor. We define a Teenvestor as a teenager who has invested time, skill, or resources in one or more of the following activities:

1. buying or selling stocks, mutual funds, bonds, and other financial assets;

2. running his or her own profit-making business;

3. starting business activities motivated by social or environmental concerns;

4. advancing the use of his or her own inventions;

5. engaging in charitable activities to help other people outside of his or her immediate family; or

6. engaging in other activities to explore his or her passions.

In this book, we focus on the activities of Teenvestors who want to invest in stocks, bonds, and other financial assets. Most aspiring Teenvestors have neither the money nor the time necessary to become millionaires overnight in the stock and mutual fund markets. With a bit of knowledge, however, Teenvestors can make a good amount of money if they steadily invest in good companies for the long term. Over time, you too can start putting your money away in strong companies and get a financial head start on your peers.

It is easy to get wrong ideas about how money is made in the stock market if you listen to the news or read the headlines. The media would have you believe the stock market is just giving money away. Some people have indeed made money in fast-growing technology stocks, but many have also lost money by buying high and then watching their share prices fall to new lows. Just don't believe all the hype.

No one is born knowing how to invest. Some people try to learn investing by just diving into stocks or mutual funds without understanding the basics. When they try to learn investing this way, they can lose their savings quickly. You, on the other hand, are lucky enough to be living at a time when you can easily get the basic knowledge to become a good, steady investor.

What are the advantages of learning how to invest at a young age? First, you will get ahead of all your peers. While your friends are worrying about affording the latest device or fashion, you will be investing in their manufacturers. While your classmates are setting aside their holiday gift money for a new game system, you will be stashing money away for the future, when you might accumulate enough cash by selling your stocks or mutual funds to pay for a car, a computer, your education, and other items that will last a lot longer than those gadgets

Investment principles learned early will stay with you forever. When you start to appreciate how money grows by earning interest on interest (also known as *compounding*) and by investing long-term in stocks and mutual funds, you will realize that a little money invested today can produce much more tomorrow.

WHY INVEST IN THE STOCK MARKET?

For most people, investment choices include stocks (and stock mutual funds), corporate bonds, and government bonds. Stocks, as you may already know, represent how much of a company an investor owns. Corporate bonds are loans investors make to corporations, and government bonds are loans investors make to the government.

Investing in the stock market, statistics show, has earned investors an annual average of about 11.4% for about the last 90 years. This is more than double the average yearly profit of 5.2% for long-term government bonds over the same period. What this says is that stocks are better than other investments if you are a long-term investor. Yes, there are bumps along the way, such as in 2008 and 2002 when stockholders lost about 36.6% and 22.0% of their investments, respectively. However, by owning stocks you will be in good company, because 52% of Americans now own stocks according to a Gallup survey.

YOUR ONE BIG ADVANTAGE

As an investor, you have one big advantage over your parents and other adults – time. The younger you are, the more time you have to invest, and this gives your investments time to grow through the power of *compounding*. As we will discuss more fully in the book, compounding is the idea that if you make a habit of reinvesting any profit you earn on your investments back into your original investment, your money will multiply before you know it. A simple example would be a $1,000 yearly deposit in a bank account (paying 10% each year in interest) for the next 50 years. If the depositor reinvested every penny of interest back into the account, she would have $13,533,293 at the end of the 50th year. If she just stuffed the money into a giant piggy bank, she would have only $50,000 (50 years x $1,000 = $50,000). We know you can't even think about your life that far in the future. However, we are trying to illustrate how steady investing over a long time can make your money multiply. And at your age, you have the time.

HOW THIS BOOK WORKS

This book is written primarily for Teenvestors, but it contains three chapters written specifically for parents: Introduction II, Chapter 2 (Helping Teenvestors Manage Money), and Chapter 22 (Taxes and Tax-Friendly Investments). We recommend that your parents also read Chapter 21 (Online Brokers) and Chapter 23 (The Teenvestor Ten), even though they are written for Teenvestors, so they can help you establish an account with a company that will assist you in buying and selling stocks and mutual funds.

This book concentrates on teaching Teenvestors how to invest in the stocks of America's biggest and most profitable companies. We also touch upon other investments related to stocks, such as mutual funds and special bonds that are appropriate for young investors.

At times, we repeat certain important concepts This is deliberate because certain ideas need to be repeated with relatable examples for Teenvestors.

In addition, some of the topics discussed in this book are for the advanced Teenvestor—one who is at least 15 years old and has been investing for two years or more. The average reader can skip these sections and still understand the ideas in the rest of the book.

On our website, www.teenvestor.com, you will find additional information about the topics in each chapter, videos related to the subjects covered in each chapter, as well as chapter assignments that help emphasize the investment concepts in the book. By the time you complete the assignments and access some of the educational materials associated with the book, you will know more about investing than most college graduates and the average adult.

TeenVestor®: The Practical Investment Guide for Teens and Their Parents and its accompanying website should be the first stop for any young person who wants to gain investment skills that will last a lifetime. No one can learn all he needs to know about investing from one source, but this book can get you started. Just read patiently, use the information resources we provide, and begin investing in solid companies right away!

For more information and website links associated with this introduction, please visit:

www.teenvestor.com/introduction

INTRODUCTION II
(for Parents)

TeenVestor®: The Practical Investment Guide for Teens and Their Parents is our solution to the lack of investment education for the very young on how to become lifelong investors.

The word Teenvestor, used throughout this book, is generally defined as a teenager who has invested his or her time, skill, or resources in one or more of the following activities:

1. buying or selling stocks, mutual funds, bonds, and other financial assets;

2. running his or her own profit-making business;

3. starting business activities motivated by social or environmental concerns;

4. advancing the use of his or her own inventions;

5. engaging in charitable activities to help other people outside of his or her immediate family; or

6. engaging in other activities to explore his or her passions.

In this book, we focus on the activities of Teenvestors who want to invest in stocks, mutual funds, bonds, and other financial assets. Along with a companion website, www.teenvestor.com, *TeenVestor* breaks new ground in that it considers investment education as a normal part of the education process of young people.

TeenVestor was written with the understanding that the young need survival skills different from those required just 30 years ago. They face the prospect of diminished social safety nets (such as reduced Social Security benefits and welfare), the task of managing more of their retirement funds on their own, and the likelihood that they will have to shoulder more of their own educational and medical expenses as the government and companies implement new budget cuts. These realities make it imperative that children learn ways to make their money grow, no matter how small the initial amount. By exposing their children to stocks, mutual funds, and other financial instruments at an early age, parents lay the foundation for their children to become savvy adult investors.

PARENTAL HOPES AND DREAMS

Some parents today recognize that their children should learn how to save and invest. More than ever, they are concerned about their children's financial future, and they realize that reading, 'riting and 'rithmetic are no longer sufficient to guarantee a decent standard of living. Indeed, financial experts agree that young people need greater financial skills than their parents did to survive the economic challenges of their adulthood.

Brokerage firms have noticed the desire of some parents to teach their children about investing. A number of companies are moving to capture the potential investing power in this country, and thereby expand their market reach to a new group of investors with whom they can build long-term relationships.

To encourage young people to invest early, and thereby gain their lifetime loyalty, new low-fee investment models have emerged. For example, companies such as Betterment, Wealthfront, and TradeKing Advisors have introduced low-fee services that use technology to automatically invest for clients, based on how much they want to earn and how widely they want to diversify their investments. These types of companies, as well as low-cost stock trading firms, are making investing more accessible to young people with modest amounts of cash.

HISTORICAL LACK OF INVESTMENT EDUCATION

Unfortunately, not all parents appreciate the need to help their children become Teenvestors, nor can they easily find age-appropriate resources. If you do have a slight interest in boosting your children's financial acumen, you probably won't get much help from your children's schools. A report by the Council for Economic Education, titled *Survey of the States: Economic and Personal Finance Education in Our Nation's States*, showed that only 19 states required a personal finance course to be offered to students from K-12, and only 24 states required an economics class in high school. An article by Money.com about the report had this to say about the lack of comprehensive economic education in our school system:

Young adults have been shown to have particularly low levels of financial acumen; they are most prone to expensive credit behaviors like payday loans and paying interest and late fees on credit card balances. This behavior, combined with soaring student debt, often puts them in a financial bind before they earn their first paycheck. A little financial education, the evidence now shows, may go a long way.

REASONS PARENTS DON'T ENCOURAGE YOUNG INVESTORS

Investing is a good habit that can be learned at an early age. Regular investors end up saving far more than occasional investors, even when they regularly invest a small amount at a time. The most important thing about investing, however, is that time is your friend – the earlier a person starts, the better off that person will be in the long run. And time is a good friend of Teenvestors, most of who will retire in about 50 to 60 years.

Unfortunately, however, the typical investor is a 45-year-old man. What about all those with the power of youth behind them? Why shouldn't young people learn that they too can make their money grow? As with most things in life, parents have a big influence on their children's savings and investment habits. Parents have to step up and introduce their children to the lifelong journey of money management.

In our research, we have found that there are five major reasons parents shy away from encouraging their children to start investing early: (1) Parents themselves don't know much about investing; (2) Parents think their children can't understand investing concepts; (3) Parents fear their children might put too much emphasis on money;

(4) Parents think that teaching their children about investing will interfere with their basic education (the three R's); and (5) Parents think investing skills will come naturally with maturity.

Parents Themselves Don't Know Much About Investing

To many parents, investing can be quite confusing and intimidating. For one thing, it looks so mysterious. All that jargon such as earnings per share, leverage, price-earnings ratios, dividend yields, and others is enough to intimidate any individual looking for a basic understanding of investments. Then there is the myth that investing requires great mathematical acumen. With all these perceived barriers to becoming an investor, many people choose to stay out of the markets completely or let the "experts" handle their money, at great expense, we might add. But what you don't know is that many brokers don't have more than high school diplomas. What they do have, however, is experience, which they gain by essentially advising you on what stocks, bonds, and mutual funds you should buy.

Onc of the problems with turning everything over to the so-called financial experts is that you don't learn anything about investing. What this means is that you will always be dependent on brokers who are probably no smarter than you are. It also means that you have no knowledge about investing that you can pass on to your children (except perhaps, to advise them to get a stock broker). But an old African proverb says: "A man's morning begins whenever he wakes up during the day." Translation: it is never too late to wake up and start changing your attitudes and behavior. Starting with this book, you can learn investment basics so you can help your children become Teenvestors.

Parents Feel Their Children Can't Understand Investing Concepts

Most of you have probably heard of Junior Achievement – an organization established in 1919 that reaches about 11 million young students around the world to help them with financial literacy, entrepreneurship, and work readiness. However, there are other organizations that teach high school students about financial literacy such as: DECA, which reaches more than 250,000 young students, and whose mission is to prepare emerging leaders in finance, marketing, and other work-related skills; the Securities Industry and Financial Markets Association, which runs the Stock Market Game, a stock market learning tool and contest for aspiring young investors; Young Americans Center for Financial Education, which since 1984 has been running the Young Americans Bank and has a mission to teach children about money; and many more that have successfully taught young people investment basics. All of these organizations have proven that young people are indeed capable of absorbing financial and investment concepts when these are properly communicated. See our website, www.teenvestor.com/introduction1, for a list of organizations that teach young people about money and investing.

We have personally experienced the ease with which young people can pick up clearly presented investment concepts. For years, we ran a camp called Teen Business Camp in which 14- to 17-year-olds spent two weeks on a college campus to learn about the stock market and entrepreneurship. One year we established a stock portfolio with Merrill Lynch & Co. and tracked the results daily, noting any economic news that affected the portfolio. The Teenvestors graduated from the program with a working knowledge of the stock market – much more knowledge than an average 21-year-old college graduate.

Parents Fear Their Children Might Put Too Much Emphasis on Money

To ensure that Teenvestors establish healthy money habits without being obsessed with money, parents should continue the moral lessons they teach daily. Teaching your Teenvestors investment concepts is only one of the ways to ensure that they are prepared for the financial stresses they will encounter in adulthood. The reality is that your children will have to learn about money one way or another, with or without your help. You can make sure they put money and investing in perspective – neither making it the most important thing in their lives nor ignoring the benefits of saving and investing. Without your help, they will grow up unprepared for financial difficulties they may face at some point in their lives.

Parents Feel That Teaching Their Children About Investing Will Interfere With Their Basic Education

We believe that investment skills are as important as the basic academic skills students learn in school. We hold this view because of the vast changes in the American economy in the past few decades. For one, stability in the workforce has disappeared. There are no more job guarantees, and this means that as adults, your children may face financial droughts unless they know how to save and invest. In addition, consider these possibilities: young people face the prospects of receiving less financial aid for their education, diminished social safety nets (such as reduced Social Security benefits and welfare), managing more of their retirement funds on their own than you do now, and shouldering more of their own medical expenses. These realities make it imperative that your children learn more than how to read, write, and do calculus. They also have to know about growing whatever amount of money they have.

Richard Fairbank, Chairman and CEO of Capital One Financial Corporation, sums it up nicely in the Council for Economic Education's *Survey of the States* report cited earlier:

> Recent economic challenges have highlighted the importance of teaching our kids to understand personal finance. The day-to-day relevance of economic concepts and financial responsibility will only continue to increase as the world is rapidly transformed by science and technology. Providing students with the practical tools they need to apply that knowledge will help them succeed financially by creating businesses, driving innovation, and achieving personal dreams. Working together, we can infuse our classrooms with the necessary foundational capabilities and make financial education a centerpiece of our public and private agenda.

Parents Think Investing Skills Will Come Naturally With Maturity

Hoping that the young will pick up investment skills as they get older is wishful thinking. We firmly believe that money management skills are similar to other skills such as learning how to play tennis or the piano. Children don't just magically know how to play tennis by watching Wimbledon. They have to hammer away at the ball on the court under the watchful eye of someone who can teach them how to swing. Tiger Woods, one of the greatest golfers who ever lived, started swinging golf clubs at the age of four. There is no question that the earlier one begins to learn a skill, the better. In addition, if you let your children learn how to manage money by trial and error, they may never learn that saving and investing should be a lifelong habit.

ENCOURAGING GIRLS TO INVEST

For parents of daughters, we have a special message: don't shortchange them when it comes to instruction about money and investing. Gone are the days when girls waited for Mr. Right to marry them and support them forever. The truth is that today's women (yes, even your grown-up little girl) may stay single longer, have their own careers, outlive their husbands (if they marry), and get divorced. In addition, because money can be a source of control and power, it is necessary that women know how to manage and invest it. Teaching girls about investing will help them face challenges and opportunities encountered by women in our society.

If we haven't yet convinced you about the importance of teaching your girls about investing, keep in mind that some of the smartest financial experts are women, even though women are still underrepresented on Wall Street. Abby Joseph Cohen, head of the Global Markets Institute at Goldman Sachs, can actually move the financial markets when she issues her opinions. Blythe Masters, former head of commodities at J.P. Morgan, was responsible for an innovative financial instrument called a credit default swap. Ruth Porat is currently the Chief Financial Officer at Alphabet and was also the Chief Financial Officer and Executive Vice President of Morgan Stanley at one point in her career. Though they are fewer in number than their male counterparts, there are many more women like these who have proven they have a lot to offer Wall Street and the rest of the financial industry.

Beyond Wall Street, there are plenty of examples of women who have demonstrated the business and financial savvy to run large companies. The following executives come to mind: IBM Chairman and CEO Ginni Rometty; PepsiCo Chairman and CEO Indra Nooyi; General Motors Chairman and CEO Mary T. Barra; Hewlett-Packard Chairman and CEO Meg Whitman; Facebook COO Sheryl Sandberg; Yahoo CEO and President Marissa Mayer; and YouTube CEO Susan Wojcicki. These women, together with "women of Wall Street," can serve as role models for your Teenvestors.

ENCOURAGING MINORITIES TO INVEST

A report by the Urban Institute titled *Nine Charts About Wealth Inequality in America* illustrated the differences between the wealth of whites and black and Hispanic families. Wealth is a total of a family's assets such as savings, real estate, business, and investments less its debt. By contrast, income is generally related to wages and money from dividends and government benefits. In general, wealth is built over a long period – sometimes over generations.

The Urban Institute report indicated that the median white family has $134,230 in wealth, while African-American and Hispanic families have only $11,030 and $13,730 respectively. The main reasons for this disparity are 1) lower levels of home ownership among blacks and Hispanics, 2) lower incomes among blacks and Hispanics compared with whites, and 3) lower participation rates for blacks and Hispanics in retirement investment accounts, which are a significant way to build wealth through the ownership of stocks, bonds, and other financial assets.

The Great Recession, which lasted from approximately December 2007 to June 2009, helped reveal the significance of the stock market in the economic recovery that followed. The Pew Research Center reports the following:

> White households are much more likely than minority households to own stocks directly or indirectly through retirement accounts. Thus, they were in better position to benefit from the recovery in financial markets.

If you are a minority, starting your children early on investing can help them feel more comfortable putting their money in stocks – one of the best assets for building wealth in the long run.

African-American parents can point their Teenvestors to some prominent Wall Street and business role models such as: TIAA-CREF President and CEO Roger Ferguson; BET Chairman and CEO Debra L. Lee; J.C. Penny CEO Marvin Ellison; American Express Chairman and CEO Kenneth I. Chenault; Xerox Chairman and CEO Ursula M. Burns; Credit Suisse CEO Tidjane Thiam; and Merck Chairman and CEO Kenneth C. Frazier.

Perhaps one of the most significant, iconic African-American financiers and entrepreneurs over the past 50 years is Reginald F.

Lewis. Mr. Lewis bought Beatrice International Foods for $985 million in 1987, and the company subsequently became the first black-owned company to exceed $1 billion in sales. Unfortunately, he died in 1993 at the age of 50, but African-Americans who wish to operate at the highest level in the financial world should explore his path to success and his philanthropic endeavors. Young African-Americans should read his book, *Why Should White Guys Have All the Fun?* for inspiration.

Top Hispanic business leaders include United Airlines President and CEO Oscar Muñoz; Express Scripts Chairman and CEO George Paz; ADP President and CEO Carlos Rodriguez; GameStop CEO J. Paul Raines; and Ryder Systems Inc. Chairman and CEO Robert E. Sanchez.

We recommend that you start looking for role models in some of the general business publications we list in Chapter 11. You can also find a list of publications and organizations, complete with links, on our website, www.teenvestor.com.

THE BEST INVESTMENT FOR TEENVESTORS

Now that we have convinced you that teaching your children how to invest is important, what type of investment should they make with their money? The typical investor has three investment choices: stocks (including their employer's investment incentives), corporate bonds, and government bonds. (Mutual funds and exchange-traded funds are largely made up of a stocks and/or bonds.)

Historically, stocks have had an advantage over corporate bonds and government bonds. For the past 90 years, stocks and government bonds have returned an average of 11.4% and 5.2%, respectively. More than 80 million people in the United States participate in the stock market in one way or another.

While there are no foolproof investments, investing in the stock market is more profitable and more appropriate for children than is investing in bonds, real estate, and other assets that require a lot of money.

HOW YOU CAN HELP YOUR TEENVESTOR

This book is written primarily for Teenvestors, but it contains three chapters written specifically for you: this introduction, Chapter 2 (Helping Teenvestors Manage Money), and Chapter 22 (Taxes and Tax-Friendly Investments). We recommend, also, that you read Chapter 21 (Online Brokers) and Chapter 23 (The Teenvestor Ten) so you can help your Teenvestor choose and establish an online trading account and navigate websites that can help them understand the basics of investing. If you are a novice investor yourself, perhaps you should read the entire book so you can better help your Teenvestor and yourself.

The book concentrates on teaching Teenvestors how to invest in the stocks of America's biggest companies. We also touch upon other investments related to stocks such as mutual funds. In addition, we mention how Teenvestors can invest in certificates of deposit (CDs) and zero-coupon bonds (which include U.S. Savings Bonds).

In some sections of the book, we point your Teenvestor to our website, www.teenvestor.com, for more details about the ideas we are teaching them. On our website, they will also find links to other good investment websites, videos, and other educational material.

Some sections of the book direct your Teenvestor to online assignments at teenvestor.com, which also contains the solutions to the assignments. When she completes these assignments, your Teenvestor will know more about investing than most college graduates.

> For more information and website links associated with this introduction, please visit:
>
> www.teenvestor.com/introduction

1

GETTING AND MANAGING MONEY

Advising Teenvestors on how to invest without telling them how to get money to do so is pointless. In this chapter, we explore your choices for getting and saving money to put in stocks, mutual funds, or any other financial investment.

You have only three ways to get the money you need for investing: from your parents and relatives, from a job, and from your own business. We will discuss these three options in this chapter.

MONEY FROM PARENTS AND RELATIVES

Many of the Teenvestors we've met get most of their investment money from their parents and relatives. This money includes cash gifts, allowance, and money for certain chores done around the house. If you receive no regular allowance from your parents, you can start campaigning for one now. But you should show that you can be responsible with the money they give you. We have some suggestions to prove to them you are mature enough to do it.

Propose an Allowance Figure

You can show you're serious about saving and investing by proposing an allowance figure. If you currently receive an allowance, the technique we suggest will make sure the amount is appropriate for your needs. Forget about telling your parents about your friend's big allowance. That won't work. The only thing that will work is for you to carefully think about your own needs and match them with the amount you request.

Before you can propose an allowance figure (and be on your way to becoming a good Teenvestor), you must learn how to create a *budget*. This is a way to show how you spend or save the money you get each week or month from your parents, relatives, a job, or other sources such as your own business.

The Family Budget

Your parents probably create a budget for your family each month. Your family's budget will include your parents' total monthly salary and expenses such as rent or *mortgage* (payments on your parents' house loan) and other items. Table 1.1 shows an example of a family's monthly budget. Notice that the first item on the table is *income*, or the money the family keeps after paying taxes on its salary.

TABLE 1.1
Monthly Budget Example for a Family

Income
  1. Monthly Salary (after taxes) $4,680

    TOTAL INCOME   **$4,680**

Expenses

1.	Rent or Mortgage	$1000
2.	Electricity/Gas/Oil	$200
3.	Family Cell Phone Plan	$150
4.	Cable, Internet Service	$150
5.	Water	$30
6.	Property Tax	$100
7.	Household Items	$150
8.	Food	$800
9.	Car Payments	$500
10.	Car Insurance	$100
11.	Education for Children	$400
12.	Credit Card Payments	$200
13.	Savings & Investments	$400
14.	Gifts	$100
15.	Recreation	$100
16.	Vacation Money	$300
17.	Other	$100

    TOTAL EXPENSES   **$4,680**

Expense items 1 to 10 on Table 1.1 are some of the expenses that most families must pay each month. If the family does not pay its rent or mortgage, it will find itself homeless. If the family does not make its credit card payments, it will have credit card companies calling to demand payment.

The next expense item on the list (expense item 12) is "Savings & Investments." Experts recommend that each family always put money aside for savings and investments after covering "must-pay" bills such as mortgage and rent. These experts refer to setting aside savings and investment amounts as "paying yourself first." After Savings & Investments, you will see other expenses that are somewhat less important.

Items such as gifts, recreation, and vacation are nice, but they can be eliminated from the budget if the family needs extra money immediately. These types of expenses are called *discretionary expenses*. Eliminating gifts, for example, may make family members unhappy, but it may be necessary if a parent loses his or her job.

Some expenses are not monthly expenses. For example, some families put aside money each month for a once-a-year vacation. They spread this once-a-year expense over 12 months to avoid having to come up with a lump sum for a vacation. As an example, let's say that a vacation will cost a family $2,400. This means that if the family has a whole year to put aside money for the trip, $200 will have to be put aside each month. The calculation is as follows:

Monthly Amount = Amount / (# of Months to Pay for It)

In our example, the "Amount" is $2,400, and the "# Of Months to Pay for It" is the number of months the family will save before accumulating enough cash for the trip – 12 months. The "Monthly Amount" is then equal to:

$$\$2,400 \: / \: 12 \text{ months} = \$200 \text{ per month}$$

The numbers on Table 1.1 won't match what your parents make or spend, but the table itself will show some of the categories of expenses your parents may have to meet each month. By the way, not all parents like to tell their children exactly how much they make or spend.

Your Own Budget

One thing always holds true for budgets: money that comes into your hands (or income) should be equal to the money you spend paying for things and on "Savings & Investments." The equation can be written like this:

$$\text{Money You Get} = \text{Money You Spend on Paying for Things}$$
$$+ \text{ Money Set Aside for "Savings \& Investments"}$$

Your first step is to write down all the things you spend money on and the things your parents buy for you. These items should fall into three groups:

1. Small items that you buy or pay for on a weekly basis like school lunches, snacks, or bus money. If you pay for some of these items daily, add them up to show the weekly amount.

2. Small amounts you ask from your parents for leisure activities or hobbies such as going to the movies, to laser tag, to the pizzeria, etc.

3. Purchases such as shoes, clothes, electronics and other big-ticket items that you or your parents pay for every once in a while.

Worksheet 1.1 is for you to write down your weekly income and weekly expenses. This should include the items in groups 1 and 2. If you are also responsible for buying items in group 3, include those as well.

On the income side, you have several ways of getting money: from parents and relatives, from a job, or from a business you run.

Unlike the family budget, your personal budget should be for weekly amounts. You can also prepare a worksheet for monthly expenses if you'd like, but we think that weekly is the way to go because most parents give weekly allowances to their children.

Make sure that each item you put on the worksheet is reasonable. Remember that you will use this worksheet to ask your parents for a fair allowance if they can afford to give you money each week.

The purpose of creating this budget is to show your parents that you are serious about handling more of your own expenses. This is a very important step, because before your parents can trust you with more cash, they have to be sure that you can budget it wisely. Notice that the third expense item on Worksheet 1.1 is "Savings & Investments." Once again, savings and investments should be listed

Worksheet 1.1
Weekly Budget Example for Teenvestors

Income
1.   Money From Parents $
2.   Money From Relatives $
3.   Money From A Job $
4.   Money From A Business $

   TOTAL INCOME $_____

Expenses
   1. School Lunch $
   2. Other School Items $

   3. Savings & Investments $

   4. Gas (if you drive) $
   5. Snacks $

   6. Long-Term Goal $
   7. Short-Term Goal $
   8. Other Item #1 $
   9. Other Item #2 $
   10. Other Item #3 $
   11. Other Item #4 $
   12. Other Item #5 $

   TOTAL EXPENSES $_____

after the items that a person *must* pay. Please don't ever put savings and investments last on your list. We think it belongs close to the top for teens, since their parents provide most of the things they need for survival, like rent or food.

The two lines, "Long-Term Goal" and "Short-Term Goal" (expense line numbers 6 and 7), need explanations. A *goal* is something you are trying to achieve. For example, your goal for the next two weeks could be to read a book cover-to-cover. Your parents' goal could be to learn Italian for a vacation in Europe next year.

You can have social goals (such as learning a language), political goals (such as becoming your class president), educational goals (college), financial goals (such as investing in stocks within one month), and other goals. In this book, of course, we are concentrating on financial goals.

You can have long-term goals or short-term goals. Long-term goals are things you want to accomplish in a year or more. Short-term goals are things you want to accomplish in a matter of days, weeks, or months.

Your budget already includes your savings and investment goals. But what about goals to buy a computer or video game? A computer costing several hundred dollars will probably be considered a long-term goal. A game will probably be in the short-term-goal category unless it costs more than $50 or so.

If, for example, you want to spend no more than $1,000 for a computer, you may have to spread the purchase over one year to save enough. To get the weekly amount you would have to save, divide $1,000 by the 52 weeks in a year. This amounts to:

$1,000 / 52 weeks = $19.23 per week

So on your weekly budget, you should insert $19.23 per week in the Long-Term Goal line (expense line 6). If you create a monthly budget instead of a weekly budget, the amount for the Long-Term Goal will be calculated as follows:

$1,000 / 12 months = $83.33 per month

Short-term goals are treated the same way – you divide the amount by the number of weeks or months in which you hope to gather enough money to buy the item.

The way to use this worksheet is to do the following:

1. Monthly or weekly budget – you decide. We recommend that you list weekly expenses.

2. Fill out the expense section of the table.

3. Sum up all the expenses to see the total amount you plan to spend each period.

4. If you don't receive an allowance from your parents, show them your expenses and ask them if they can afford to give you money each week (or month) to cover them. Ask for suggestions on what to drop from your expense list if they can't afford or aren't willing to give you the money you need. If your expenses are reasonable, and they can afford it, you may find that they give you the sum you request.

5. If you are getting an allowance, ask them to adjust it based on your "Savings & Investments" category. You may want to tell them that you'd like to buy a share of stock (that costs between $30 and $50) every month or two after you read the rest of this book.

6. Using the numbers you filled in on Worksheet 1.1, ask your parents to let your relatives know that, as a Teenvestor, you are ready to accept cash gifts for investing in stocks or mutual funds.

7. If you are old enough to work (in some areas that means you are 16 or older), ask your parents to allow you to work so that you can earn income that will cover your expenses, and for savings and investments. We will discuss this later in the chapter.

8. If you have any special skills or hobbies, see if you can use them to make money by starting your own business. We will discuss this further.

9. If all else fails, and you can't get your parents to give you the allowance to cover your expenses (including your savings and investments), don't panic. Keep reading the book and you will dazzle them enough by what you know about investing in stocks that they will eventually give in (if they can afford to do so).

Allowance & Budgeting Tools at Your Disposal

You can create and manage your budget the old school way by entering your expenses and cash on a spreadsheet and periodically updating them. However, as technology advances, mobile apps are becoming popular tools for Teenvestors to handle living allowances and everyday financial matters like organizing expenses, managing automatic bill paying services, and receiving direct deposits.

There are quite a few apps that are extremely useful for managing money. Some just help you see and allocate where you spend your money and alert you when you are violating any set limits. Others are a lot more sophisticated and can connect to your bank account using the same encryption and security systems used by banking institutions. However, you'll need to share passwords to your financial accounts to use the services that access them. Although the apps track and update data about your income and transactional history, they do not have the ability to move your money without your consent.

At this writing, some of the popular budgeting apps to help you manage your allowance and finances include: Mint, Level Money, Acorns, LearnVest, Tykoon, PennyOwl, iAllowance, ChoreMonster, Digit, and many more. Our website, www.teenvestor.com/chapter1, is kept up to date with links to more allowance and budgeting apps.

Convincing Your Parents You Are Responsible With Money

Most parents who can afford to don't mind giving their children an allowance, as long as they know that the money will be used responsibly. The best thing you can do is to help your parents build trust in you. You have taken the first step already by learning how to create a budget. The other way you can get your parents to trust your judgment in handling money is to ask them for more responsibility to make purchases on your own – not just small items, but also the more expensive things you need. Here is an example of how one young person did this to get her parents to trust her more with money. At the beginning of summer, this girl asked her parents to give her some of the money that she knew they would have to spend on her clothes for the next school year. She put that money in her savings account, and at the end of the summer she produced the money and went shopping with her parents. This may seem like no big deal to you, but think about what this budding Teenvestor actually accomplished. By asking her parents for the money, she has shown that she cares that they know she can be trusted not to spend the money on stupid stuff. By bringing it out for the shopping trip, she has proven that she can indeed be responsible with her parents' money.

Asking to hold some of the money that your parents intend to spend on you is always a good way to build their trust in you when it comes to handling money. But remember that the first time you misuse that money, you ruin your chances of getting a reasonable allowance or money to invest.

WORKING FOR MONEY AT HOME

Besides asking for an allowance, another way to get money is to work for it. You can work around the house by doing extra chores for your parents. Please understand that we are not talking about chores you should be doing anyway such as keeping your room clean or vacuuming the living room floor. We are referring to tasks that are above what your parents expect you to do for the family. For example, if your parents expect you to mow the lawn every two weeks during the summer, you shouldn't consider that an extra chore for which you should ask for money. On the other hand, cleaning out the garage or painting some rooms in your house may be chores for which your parents will gladly pay.

You can start by giving your parents suggestions about things you can do (besides your regular chores) to help them around the house for pay. These things should be more than little items such as running errands. They should be meaningful things and they should require real, but safe work. Don't bother volunteering for things you are too young to do or for which you have no real experience. For example, unless you are at least 14 years old, don't ask to paint the exterior of your house; you are too young to climb ladders, and your hands may not be strong enough to properly complete the job.

GETTING A REAL JOB

Even if you are lucky enough to get an allowance from your parents or you are able to get money for doing chores around the house, there will come a time when you want to make your own money – enough to invest in stocks and mutual funds, and enough to meet some of your long-term and short-term goals.

While this is not a book on how to get a job, there are a few things you need to know about finding employment. First, don't think about working unless you are 16 or older. Second, if you are thinking about a job, you need a résumé. A professional-looking résumé will set you apart from the rest of your peers for any job you seek. See our website, www.teenvestor.com, for more information on résumé writing.

At your age, you may be able to get a job at a fast food restaurant or coffee shop. However, we recommend that you seek work that rewards you for how much effort you put forth. Whatever job you get, remember when you get your first paycheck to "pay yourself first" by saving or investing some money. Make this a priority, or the money you get will be quickly wasted.

STARTING YOUR OWN BUSINESS

Teenvestors have come a long way from running lemonade stands. These days, you are likely to find young entrepreneurs running full-fledged businesses that range from building apps to manufacturing clothing and other items for sale to a wide range of customers. One benefit of starting your own business is that it can help provide you with the money to start investing in stocks and mutual funds.

Since this book does not focus on teaching entrepreneurship, we point you to our website, www.teenbusiness.com, and our twitter handle, @teenmogul, which provide many examples of teen entrepreneurs and will teach you how to start your own business. You may also be interested in our most recent list of top teen entrepreneurs found at www.teenbusiness.com/top20.

OPENING AN ACCOUNT

Before you can begin saving money, you need a place to put your money. You can stash your money in your house, but if you do so, you will be tempted to use it. The best solution is to put your money in a bank.

Fortunately, some new online-only banks such as BankMobile, Simple, and Moven are charging little or no fees for maintaining small balances in checking and savings accounts. In addition, these banks have eliminated or drastically reduced exorbitant overdraft fees which have become a big source of profit for the traditional banks.

One of the disadvantages of an online-only bank is that you will probably not be able to get 24/7 full service support from an operator. Another disadvantage is that you may not have access to as many automated teller machines (ATMs) for withdrawals and deposits as with traditional banks.

Some of the traditional banks such as Bank of America, J.P. Morgan Chase, Citibank, Capital One, and Wells Fargo are trying to keep pace with the online-only banks so they too have been focusing on eliminating or reducing fees and providing easy-to-use apps for mobile banking. We recommend that you look into both the online-only banks and the traditional banks because the bank you choose will depend on your needs. In Chapter 23, we provide The Teenvestor Ten for Banking, which is our list of the most Teenvestor-friendly banks.

For more information, website links, videos, and any assignments associated with this chapter, please visit:

www.teenvestor.com/chapter1

TeenVestor

2

HELPING TEENVESTORS
MANAGE MONEY
(FOR PARENTS)

Parents go to great lengths to make sure their children receive the best education that money can buy. They send their children to music lessons, ballet lessons, tennis lessons, computer summer camps, and other skill-intensive programs and activities. Unfortunately, they neglect one of the most inexpensive and valuable skills their children can acquire – how to handle money. In a capitalist system, as we have here in the United States, knowing how to manage the money one earns is of utmost importance.

A report titled *Money Matters on Campus*, conducted by EverFi and sponsored by Higher One (a financial aid disbursement company), summarized the results of a survey of the financial know-how of 42,000 college freshmen. The survey showed that on average, the students could only answer about one-third of the questions relating to budgeting and credit issues.

Sometimes parents neglect to teach their children about money because they were brought up in families that kept financial matters secret or discouraged their children's participation in decisions involving money. Parents raised in such environments are in turn applying the same flawed principles to raising their own children. The problem is that the amount of income at the disposal of the average teen aged 15 to 17 is about $5,000, according to a survey by Marketingvox and the Rand Youth Poll . This figure includes the wages they earn by working outside of the home. Without proper lessons about money management at an early age, that income will quickly be spent unwisely.

Learning the basics of how to handle money is the first step in your children's financial education. Early financial literacy will arm your Teenvestors with the knowledge they need to start investing in the stock market, mutual funds, and other financial assets.

While not many Teenvestors will earn great sums of money by investing, most will still have to know how to collect money, budget it, and invest it.

The best time for young people to acquire money management skills is long before they even start investing in any financial instrument. Parents must shoulder the responsibility for ensuring that their children learn the basics of handling money in these early years. By their teen years, young people should already demonstrate the financial savvy necessary to invest in the stock market.

TEACHING MONEY MANAGEMENT

There are three common approaches parents take to help their children become financially literate: giving their children money on an as-needed basis, paying their children for doing chores, and giving their children regular allowances.

Giving Money on an As-Needed Basis

Giving children money as the need arises is one approach that all parents have taken at one time or another. For example, if your daughter wants to go to the movies with her friends and she asks you for the cash, you give her the exact sum she needs. For some purchases your child makes, giving out money this way is probably okay. Unless you trust your Teenvestor's spending habits, you wouldn't want to give her money too far in advance of purchasing big-ticket items like school clothes or a computer. The one drawback to giving money on an as-needed basis is that it doesn't help your Teenvestor learn how to budget her money or make decisions about how to use that money in the future.

Tying Allowances to Chores

Another approach some parents take in introducing their children to money management is to tie allowances to specific chores. For example, parents might assign a dollar value to taking out the garbage, mowing the lawn, vacuuming the house, and other ordinary chores that young people would normally do (without compensation) as a member of a family. Using this approach, parents frequently also dock their children money for neglecting to do such chores.

Unfortunately, with this approach, children learn neither responsibility nor money management skills. Instead, they learn to expect payment for things that they should be doing for free, such as cleaning their rooms, setting the dinner table, or refraining from beating on their brothers and sisters. If parents tie allowances to ordinary chores, they run the risk that their children may decide (on the days they are feeling particularly lazy) to forgo their allowances by not doing the chores. Parents should not mix the lessons about family responsibility with lessons on how to handle money.

Giving Out Regular Allowances in Advance

The third (and the best) approach parents employ in teaching their children how to manage money is to give a regular allowance. As you will see later in this chapter, an allowance must have a component that Teenvestors can spend any way they see fit (within general parameters you have set), with little or no strings attached. However, an allowance can also include amounts that have been earmarked for specific expenditures, for savings, and for investments. The maturity of each Teenvestor will determine what portion of the allowance can be made up of money she can spend any way she sees fit and what portion is earmarked for specific purposes.

In the next section, we have outlined what we call "allowance levels" based on your Teenvestor's maturity and the level of responsibility you feel she can handle. But before you move on to this section, we want to point out the two biggest mistakes parents make in setting allowances for their children: setting allowances based on what other children in the neighborhood get from their parents, and setting allowances based on what they themselves got from their parents when they were young.

Parents who set allowances according to the amounts given by other parents relinquish their right to determine the money that is appropriate for their children. In addition, these parents may find they can't afford to dispense the same amount of money to their children as the neighbors give to theirs.

Your own childhood allowances would probably be laughable in today's economic environment. Keep this in mind: over 20 years, inflation can triple or quadruple prices for recreational activities. Even a movie ticket can now cost $10 in some areas of the country. This is probably two to three times the price you paid as a teenager.

A prudent way to set an allowance is to take a survey of the recreational activities for which your Teenvestor may need money, and reasonable expenses for items necessary for well-being and growth. We describe how to do this in the next section.

THE FOUR ALLOWANCE LEVELS

There are four allowance levels you can dispense to your Teenvestor. Each level reflects increasing financial responsibility to help you gradually teach her how to handle money.

The Level 1 Allowance

The *Level 1 Allowance* is the basic amount we feel any Teenvestor should receive, regardless of how much she knows about managing her money. It is the basis for teaching a Teenvestor to take on more responsibility in this regard.

Worksheet 2.1 is a budget worksheet that we provided your Teenvestor in the previous chapter. We will explain some of the components of the budget as we proceed to lay out the four levels of allowances.

A reasonable Level 1 Allowance would consist of money for *discretionary expenses*. Discretionary expenses are for recreational or other activities that can easily be eliminated from a budget without severely affecting your quality of life. For example, in your family's budget, a discretionary expense could be the yearly family vacation. Your children may be disappointed, but if money gets tight you can abandon the vacation without any long-term consequences. For Teenvestors, examples of discretionary expenses could be the cost of buying snacks from vending machines or buying electronic games. In general, discretionary expenses for your Teenvestors should consist of small amounts for leisure activities or hobbies such as going to the movies, laser tag, or the pizzeria. If you normally give them money for these activities when they need it, why not bundle the money and give it to them once a week, once every two weeks, or even once a month?

Of all the allowance levels mentioned in this section, Level 1 is the only amount that should not be taken away from your Teenvestor. Whether she does her chores or not, she should continue to receive the basic allowance amount for discretionary spending as long as she continues to follow the basic moral and ethical codes you have set for its use. We want to emphasize that because this amount is discretionary, you should not tell her exactly how to spend it.

Worksheet 2.1
Weekly Budget Example for Teenvestors

Income
1.   Money From Parents $
2.   Money From Relatives $
3.   Money From A Job $
4.   Money From A Business $

   TOTAL INCOME   **$**

Expenses
1. School Lunch $
2. Other School Items $

3. Savings & Investments $

4. Gas (if you drive) $
5. Snacks $

6. Long-Term Goal $
7. Short-Term Goal $
8. Other Item #1 $
9. Other Item #2 $
10. Other Item #3 $
11. Other Item #4 $
12. Other Item #5 $

   TOTAL EXPENSES   **$**

The Level 2 Allowance

The next level of allowance that you can give your Teenvestor, if she has demonstrated that she can handle the Level 1 Allowance, is the *Level 2 Allowance*. This is the Level 1 Allowance plus some *nondiscretionary items*. These are expenses that must be paid, no matter what. In your family's budget, the nondiscretionary items could be your rent or mortgage.

When you first move your Teenvestor from Level 1 to Level 2, you should include only small, nondiscretionary items. Such items could be school lunch money (which should now be given in one lump sum), bus money and other small expenditures that may contribute to her growth and well-being.

Later, as you begin to trust her spending habits, you can add money for other nondiscretionary items, such as shoes and clothing. It could take a few months or a year before you can give her more responsibility for her nondiscretionary expenditures – it simply depends on your Teenvestor's maturity.

Once again, how much money you dispense in the Level 2 Allowance depends on your personal financial situation. The Level 2 Allowance can be taken away if your Teenvestor is not meeting your expectations on how she should spend it. When you yank her Level 2 privileges, go back to Level 1.

Some Teenvestors may not be excited about getting money in their allowances for nondiscretionary expenditures since, by definition, they have no choice as to how that money is spent; it is already earmarked. Most Teenvestors, however, will appreciate being entrusted with more responsibility in terms of more money. Even the illusion of more wealth can help Teenvestors learn about managing that wealth.

Another thing that can make nondiscretionary money more palatable for Teenvestors is that they must satisfy the Level 2 requirements before they can move to the *Level 3 Allowance,* which includes money for their savings accounts and for investments.

The Level 3 Allowance

The *Level 3 Allowance* is the Level 2 Allowance plus a savings and investments component of the budget on Worksheet 2.1 (expense line number 3). The "Savings & Investments" line is the amount of money your Teenvestor should put in a bank or invest in stocks, mutual funds, or other financial assets. It is important to note that in this category, savings really means money that is not earmarked for particular expenditures. It is money put away for emergencies. Investments represent money put into (or earmarked for) financial assets in hopes of making some interest or profit.

Budgeting experts consider the amount set aside for savings and investing as an integral part of a budget. It is so important that some call the act of setting aside money in this category "paying yourself first" – that is, once you have paid the bills that are necessary for your survival, the next thing to do is put money aside for savings and investments. Nothing else should take a higher priority. We mentioned this concept to your Teenvestor in the previous chapter, but we think you must emphasize its importance when she approaches you for an allowance.

There are steps you can take to encourage your Teenvestor to save and invest money in stocks or other financial instruments.

The first thing you can do, of course, is to give her money specifically to put in her bank account (if it is practical to establish an account) for emergency purposes or in anticipation of making investments. This, as we stated earlier, moves the Level 2 Allowance to Level 3.

Another thing you can very easily do is to set up your own money-matching program for any additional amount she puts aside in her bank account for investing. For example, if she would ordinarily put aside an additional $10 each week for savings and investments, you can add another $10 to it as long as that money will be truly used for its intended purpose.

Saving and investing are good habits to establish in your Teenvestor. Even if she does not understand the value of these habits, make her put the money in this category in the bank anyway (or put it in your own bank account on her behalf).

Because savings and investments are such important components of the allowance (and hence, the budget), you will have to periodically monitor the amount saved and invested to see if your Teenvestor is accumulating the amounts she should. Obviously, a bank account is a necessary part of this process, and you should help her open one unless she can piggy-back on your account.

The Level 3 Allowance privileges should be taken away if your Teenvestor is not meeting your expectations on how she should spend the nondiscretionary portion of the allowance. When you take away her Level 3 privileges, go back to the Level 2 amount.

The Level 4 Allowance

The *Level 4 Allowance* is the Level 3 Allowance plus "Long-Term Goal" and "Short-Term Goal" components.

Most young people seek instant pleasure. From the time they are born until they go off to college, they want immediate gratification. When they are old enough to understand the concept of money, they easily settle into compulsive buying unless their parents have taught them good money management.

One of the biggest challenges you will face is getting your Teenvestor to plan for expenditures. An important step in helping your children develop a money management plan is to have them set their own *goals*.

Goals are wants, needs and objectives your Teenvestor can set for herself. In the context of teaching Teenvestors how to manage their money, financial goals are the amounts of money put aside for specific purchases.

These goals may be long-term or short-term. While you may consider long-term goals to be objectives you hope to reach in five to ten years, teens have much shorter time frames. For a 14-year-old Teenvestor, a long-term goal could have a time horizon of one year, and a short-term goal could have a time horizon of a month.

Two important expense categories for determining your Teenvestor's allowance are "Long-Term Goals" (expense item 6) and "Short-Term Goals" (expense item 7) on Worksheet 2.1.

In the previous chapter, we advised Teenvestors to budget for short-term and long-term goals. They can do so by spreading the expenses of the items they want to buy over the period of time in which they hope to set aside sufficient money for the purchase. For example, if your Teenvestor wants to buy a $1,000 computer in a year, she has to spread the cost over a 52-week period like so:

$1,000 / 52 weeks = $19.23 per week
or
$1,000 / 12 months = $83.33 per month (if the budget is created monthly)

We consider this a long-term goal because it will take a year for your Teenvestor to save the money she needs to make the purchase. This means that on the expense side of a weekly budget, she would have to include a figure of $19.23 in the Long-Term Goals line.

Likewise, short-term purchasing goals should be spread over the period of time before the expenditure will be made. To buy a $50 item over the next two months, for example, your Teenvestor will have to spread her expenses over an 8-week period:

$50 / 8 weeks = $6.25 per week (for weekly budgets)
or
$50 / 2 months = $25 per month (for monthly budgets)

So, on the expense side of the budget (expense item 7), your Teenvestor should enter $6.25 if she creates a weekly budget or $25 if she creates a monthly budget.

The amounts for the long-term and short-term goals should be placed in a bank account, and you should be watching their accumulation.

As with other allowance levels, the Level 4 Allowance should be taken away if your Teenvestor is not meeting your expectations on how she should spend the money. When you cancel her Level 4 privileges, go back to Level 3 or Level 2.

SOURCES OF INCOME FOR YOUR TEENVESTORS

The allowance you have decided to give your Teenvestor is only one source of income in her budget. On Worksheet 2.1, the allowance to Teenvestors is listed as "Money From Parents" (income item 1). Depending on the age of your Teenvestor, you should not feel any obligation to be the sole provider of income. Remember that as long as you have decided what expenses you will pay, it is up to your Teenvestor to come up with other ways to take care of the other expenses in her budget, unless she is simply too young to come up with other income on her own. In this section, we will discuss the various other sources of money for your Teenvestor.

Money and Other Gifts From Relatives

Teenvestors receive money from grandparents, aunts and uncles for birthdays, holidays, graduations, and other special occasions and milestones. You may want to have these relatives give you the money for disbursement to your Teenvestor if you feel that she is not responsible enough to spend the money wisely. One solution is to advise these relatives to earmark some of the funds for investing in stocks, mutual funds, and other financial assets.

Relatives (including parents) can help Teenvestors start investment portfolios by giving them assets other than cash. They can give gifts such as stocks, mutual funds, bonds and other assets. These gifts can be given without adverse tax consequences for the relatives, the parents, and the Teenvestors who are the beneficiaries. Under current tax laws, gifts of less than $14,000 each year are not subject to a gift tax and thus, neither the gift givers nor the recipients are required to pay taxes on the gifts. This is known as the "gift tax exclusion." The only condition is that the recipients of the gifts must have what's called a "present interest" in the gifts. That is, the gifts must be wholly and completely available to the recipients as soon as they are actually given. Please consult a tax guide for more details on gifts.

Working Inside the Home

Another source of income for your Teenvestor to fill in the gap in her budget is money from doing extra chores around the house. Please understand that we are not talking about chores your Teenvestor should be doing anyway, such as keeping her room clean or vacuuming your living room floor. We are referring to tasks that are above and beyond your expectations of what she should be doing as a member of the family. If, for example, you expect your Teenvestor to put dirty dishes into the dishwasher every day, she should not ask you for compensation. On the other hand, it probably makes sense to pay your Teenvestor for cleaning out your garage or painting rooms in your house – difficult tasks that go beyond the mundane family chores.

Working Outside of the Home

At some point, your Teenvestor will need more money for more discretionary expenditures. The allowance you give her, the amount of money you pay her for extra chores and the amount of money from relatives will eventually fall short. She will simply need more income to meet her needs.

One way for your Teenvestor to fill this financial gap is to get a job. We feel it's a good idea for any Teenvestor who is 16 or older to seek employment. Most Teenvestors may come to that conclusion on their own because at some point, when they want more things and more discretionary money, their parents will not be able to meet their financial needs. We firmly believe, however, that the criteria for allowing your Teenvestor to work outside of the house should be that:

1. Her expenditures meet the standards you have set as acceptable in your eyes.

2. She continues a certain level of savings and investments (that is, she must continue to "pay herself first").

3. She continues to draft her weekly or monthly budget.

4. The job does not interfere with her schoolwork.

HOW TO SET THE ALLOWANCE PERIOD

The period between each allowance can vary according to how your Teenvestor handles her money. Some 13-year olds who are given an allowance monthly can make their allowances last until the end of the month, but others may spend it all in a week or a day. For children younger than 13, it is probably advisable to give weekly allowances. For older children, it depends on their maturity. If your Teenvestor cannot properly manage her money within the allowance time frame you have chosen, shorten the period between allowances.

According to child-care experts, parents should dispense allowances at designated dates and times. This gives children the opportunity to plan the activities for which they will use the discretionary portions of their allowances. Since you want your Teenvestor to learn how to properly budget for expenditures, you should not change the period between allowances without telling her in advance. In addition, you should never withhold allowance because she has misbehaved or has neglected to perform certain tasks.

THE ONGOING MONITORING OF ALLOWANCES

No allowance figure should be set in stone. You can (and should) change the allowance depending on how well your Teenvestor is handling the responsibility she has been given. The allowance can also change based on your own financial situation. If you lose your job, you may have to reduce or even eliminate the discretionary amount you are giving your Teenvestor.

One clear way of monitoring how your Teenvestor is handling the amount she is getting is to watch how she is handling her bank or investment account. If you are giving her money that she has promised to save or invest, you should see the savings accumulating in those accounts. Remember that if she is not spending money as she has outlined in her budget, you can pull away some of the allowance privileges except for the discretionary amount in the Level 1 Allowance.

ALLOWANCE & BUDGETING TOOLS AT YOUR DISPOSAL

You can help your Teenvestor create and manage her budget the old school way by entering expenses and cash on a spreadsheet and periodically updating them. However, as technology advances, mobile apps are becoming popular tools for Teenvestors to handle living allowances and everyday financial matters like organizing expenses, managing automatic bill paying services, and receiving direct deposits.

There are quite a few apps that are extremely useful for managing money. Some even help parents transfer allowance electronically to their Teenvestors and will send out alerts if they are violating any set limits. Others are a lot more sophisticated and can connect to bank accounts using the same encryption and security systems used by banking institutions.

At this writing, some of the popular allowance and budgeting apps to help you and your Teenvestor manage her allowance and finances include: Mint, Level Money, Acorns, LearnVest, Tykoon, PennyOwl, iAllowance, ChoreMonster, Digit, and many more. Our website, www.teenvestor.com/chapter1, is kept up to date with links to more allowance and budgeting apps.

For more information, website links, videos, and any assignments associated with this chapter, please visit:

www.teenvestor.com/chapter2

TeenVestor

3

INVESTMENT BASICS

We find that the best way to teach Teenvestors about stocks is to take them through the basics of a small business. Believe it or not, the most important concepts in investing in stocks can be illustrated even with a business as simple as a lemonade stand. When we ran our Teen Business Camp, we taught stock market basics by using businesses teenagers can relate to, such as a T-shirt business, a gift-basket business, or even a limousine service to illustrate all the important items to look for when evaluating the stock of a company.

In this chapter, we will use a T-shirt business to illustrate basic ideas behind stock ownership. After reading this chapter, a budding Teenvestor like you will begin to see that getting stock smart is not really that difficult.

RAISING MONEY

Susan and four other partners have decided to start their own T-shirt business, SportsTee. Her high school of 3,000 students has some of the best sports programs in the country, and her community is very supportive of high school athletics. Susan and her friends are confident that a T-shirt business will thrive in such a sports-oriented community. SportsTee will sell high quality T-shirts, painted with sports themes, at high school sporting events.

Susan and her SportsTee partners come up with a rough estimate of the amount of money they would need to start the business. They do this by figuring out how much the equipment will cost them, how many shirts they will have to purchase initially, and how much cash they will need on hand to meet initial expenses such as salary and rent, in order to keep the business running for two months before they actually start making money.

This is very similar to the way many companies determine how much cash to seek when they issue stock or borrow money. They usually figure out what they want to do – whether to start a business, expand an existing one, or buy new equipment to improve the business. The companies then issue stock or borrow money to finance these activities.

Since Susan and her friends are just starting SportsTee, their first concern is to raise enough money to buy the company's initial inventory of shirts, to purchase equipment such as buckets and paints, to pay the salaries of their helpers, and to advertise the business. As you can see from the list of expenses in Table 3.1, Susan and her

TABLE 3.1
SportsTee's Initial Start-Up Costs

(For Two Months of Operation)

1.	Cost of Raw (Unpainted) Shirts	$600
2.	Cost of Paint for Initial Purchase of Shirts	$400
3.	Brushes	$100
4.	Bucket (Highest Quality)	$120
5.	Rental of Space Per Year	$200
6.	Overalls for Painting	$150
7.	Advertising	$500
8.	Total Labor by All 5 Owners	$1,200
9.	Miscellaneous	$230
	Total Initial Cash Start-Up Costs	**$3,500**

partners calculate that they need an initial investment of $3,500 to get SportsTee off the ground. For Susan and her four partners, the next task is to figure out how to raise the $3,500 they need. They can raise the money by any one of the following methods:

1. First, Susan and her partners can invest their own $3,500 to start the company.

2. Second, SportsTee can borrow the money and pay interest to the people from whom they borrow. Susan and her partners would still be the owners of the company, except that if they don't pay the loan back, they could lose the company to the lenders.

3. Third, Susan and her partners can decide to let other investors (besides the five who started the company) put money into SportsTee to help get it going.

THE DIFFERENCE BETWEEN EQUITY AND DEBT

Susan and her four partners decide that they will each contribute $500 of their own money, making a total partner contribution of $2,500 ($500 from each of the five partners). This $2,500 figure is called *equity*. In any business, equity is the amount of money its owners contribute.

All five owners of SportsTee also decide to take out a $1,000 loan by borrowing $200 from the parents of each partner. Not surprisingly, the parents don't turn over the cash without tying a few conditions to the loan. They agree to lend SportsTee the $1,000 on the condition that (1) the loan will be repaid at an interest rate of 10% per year, (2) $600 of the borrowed funds will be repaid within one year, and (3) the other $400 will be repaid in two years. In addition, the parents warn that if SportsTee does not repay the loan in this way, the parents will either (1) take over the business or (2) if the parents feel that the business won't make it, stop giving out allowances until the money is paid back.

The $1,000 that SportsTee borrows is called debt. Debt is sometimes referred to as *short-term debt* or *long-term debt*, depending upon the length of the repayment period. Short-term debt is any amount that is to be repaid within a year. Long- term debt refers to amounts to be repaid in more than one year. Applying this rule of thumb to the borrowing, SportsTee's short-term debt is $600, while its long-term debt is $400. Furthermore, debt can be *secured* or *unsecured.* SportsTee's debt is secured because its lenders can go after whatever the company owns if the company does not pay its debts on time. Remember that Susan and her partners agree that if they fail to pay back the loan, they will have to either (1) turn over the business to their parents or (2) forgo their allowances until the money is paid back. The debt would be considered unsecured if the parents had no right to go after what the Teenvestors own if the loans are not paid back on time.

Between the $2,500 in equity that Susan and her partners contribute from their own bank accounts, and the $1,000 that they borrow from their parents, the SportsTee partners collect $3,500 to get their T-shirt business started. This combined total of equity and debt is commonly referred to as *capital.*

Public and Private Companies

Susan and her four partners are the sole owners of SportsTee. For this reason it is called a *private* company, because only Susan and her four partners (and whomever else they want to invite) are allowed to invest in the company and make decisions about its direction. Unlike SportsTee, many established companies are called *public* companies because ownership of these companies is open to the general public – anybody can invest in them. In a public company, pieces of the company, commonly known as *shares* or *stock,* are owned by *shareholders* (also known as stockholders or equity holders) or investors. One of the biggest reasons companies decide to *go public* (to offer shares of the company to the public) is that public companies can raise capital more easily. When public companies need money, they can sell investors shares in their businesses in return for cash.

Now this is where you, as a Teenvestor, would enter the picture. In public companies, equity is usually made up of *common stock, preferred stock,* and *retained earnings.*

Common stockholders not only own a piece of the company, but they also vote for the *board of directors* (the people who are responsible for overseeing the company). This means that common stockholders control the management of the company. Whether or not these investors profit from their investment depends upon how well the company performs. Common stockholders receive *dividends* – a portion of a company's profit that is distributed to stockholders.

Preferred stockholders receive dividends, but these dividends are based on a specific dollar amount of principal (similar to interest payments on loans). Preferred stockholders get paid before common stockholders get a piece of a company's profit. However, unlike common stockholders, preferred stockholders can't vote to elect the board of directors.

As you will learn later in this book, a company can do three things with the money it makes: it can distribute all its profits to its shareholders, it can keep all the money to expand the business, or it can distribute part of the money to shareholders and keep part of it to grow the company. Retained earnings are the company's profit that's put back into the company to help expand it so that it can make more money in the future.

RISK IN BUSINESS

When a company goes out of business, the people to whom the company owes money get paid before the equity holders. So if SportsTee goes broke, the partners' parents who loaned the company $1,000 get their money back first after the company sells off everything it owns, such as the buckets and the brushes, and pays any bills that it owes. Any money left over after the parents are paid back and the bills are paid goes to Susan and her four partners. So, as you can see, a lender's advantage is that she is first in line to recover a loan when things go wrong. A lender's disadvantage, on the other hand, is that she can't make more money even if the company does phenomenally well. For example, the parents who lend SportsTee money are entitled only to interest payments on their money. The investors in the business (stockholders or equity holders) are entitled to any profit the company makes (if the company decides to distribute all the profits to its stockholders). The problem for the SportsTee partners, though, is that there is no guarantee the company will make money, so they are taking a lot more *risk*. When we talk about risk in a business, we are talking about how likely that business is to lose money. The greater the chance of losing money, the higher the risk. In general, stocks are riskier than loans.

INITIAL PUBLIC OFFERINGS

Sometimes a business starts out as a private company and later becomes a public company. In general, when a private company wants to raise capital and issue stock to the public for the first time, the company sells stock through an *Initial Public Offering*, or *IPO*.

This process, commonly referred to as "going public," typically involves the following:

1. The company hires *underwriters*—investment bankers who agree to help with the IPO. The bankers can do one of two things. They can buy up all the shares the company wants to offer and then resell these shares to the public at a slightly higher price, keeping the profit. Alternatively, instead of buying up the shares from the company and then reselling them to investors, the bankers can just charge a fee to find buyers for the shares.

2. The underwriters and the company put together a *prospectus* – a document that maps out the business of the company making the IPO, its financial history, its management team, and other important information for potential investors.

3. The underwriters offer the shares to the public by putting an advertisement, called a *tombstone*, in publications.

4. The underwriters go on a visit, also known as a *road show*, with potential buyers to convince them that the stock is worth buying.

To illustrate the IPO process, let's go back to SportsTee. Assume that Susan and her partners find that the T-shirt business is a terrific idea and SportsTee is a phenomenal success. The SportsTee partners now want to expand the business to operate in other schools. Besides, Susan's parents have said that SportsTee may no longer operate in the basement of their house – the partners are making too much noise at all hours of the night, they're leaving junk all over the place, and the household grocery bill has almost doubled since SportsTee began its operations. Under these conditions, SportsTee decides to go public to raise more capital to expand its business in a larger space.

Susan approaches her friend Andy, who has lots of money and is experienced at helping companies raise money. After analyzing the situation, Andy tells Susan that he can help her go public.

Susan and Andy figure that SportsTee needs an additional $4,000 to meet its capital needs. They reach this figure by considering a number of factors, including: how much SportsTee would make each year if it were to expand, who would be running the company, how much it would cost to relocate, and the competition the company will face in the future.

Andy determines that SportsTee can find 40 Teenvestors willing to invest $100 in SportsTee for a total of $4,000. He intends to help SportsTee sell the 40 shares of stock to other investors and keep a small commission of 7% ($7 for every $100 of stock he sells) for his efforts.

To find investors who will buy the shares, Andy needs to make up a brochure to describe SportsTee, outline its financial projections, and tell how terrific the SportsTee idea is. In addition, Andy has to place an ad in the local and high school newspapers to get 40 investors.

Once Andy finds the 40 investors, sells the SportsTee shares to them and makes his $280 in commissions, he is out of the picture – he will no longer be involved in any transactions between SportsTee and its 40 investors.

What we have just illustrated is a very simplified version of an IPO. While it may be simple, we have covered some of the components of a real IPO. In the example, Andy plays the role of the underwriter, the brochure he creates is like the prospectus, and the advertisement he puts in the paper is the same as a tombstone in a real IPO. The only things that are missing here are the legal papers that have to be filed as required by the Securities and Exchange Commission, a government agency.

Recall that SportsTee has five original investors (Susan and her friends). With the 40 additional investors, it now has 45 investors in total. In real life, an IPO involves much larger companies with millions of shares offered to the public in what is referred to as a *primary market*. A primary market is the activity when shares are sold directly to the public for the first time. Once the public purchases all of these shares, anyone who wants a share will have to buy it from someone else who has bought one. These shares are sold in what is called the *secondary market*. The secondary market occurs when shares are bought from others or sold to others through people known as *brokers* who work in *stock exchanges* – places where stock is actually traded.

The concept of primary and secondary markets is important enough to go over in more detail with an example. The only time a company issuing stock benefits directly from that issuance is in the primary market – that is, when investors buy new shares issued in an IPO and give money over to that company. Later movement in the company's stock price, however, does indirectly affect the company by changing the value investors may assign to the company as a whole, thus making the company more or less valuable at any given time. An example may help better illustrate these points.

When an investor buys stock from another investor (which is the case nearly all the time), the company that initially issued the stock does not get any more money from any investor. A good example would be if your parents bought two new cars from General Motors (GM). At the time of their purchase, GM gets the money for the cars and that money helps increase its profits. But suppose your parents then sell one of the cars a few years later to a neighbor. GM is no longer in the picture, so the company will not get a piece of the money your parents get for selling their used car. In this example, buying a brand new car is much like buying shares issued in an IPO in the primary market. Selling one car a few years later is like selling shares in the secondary market. One additional wrinkle is that if the demand for GM cars increases dramatically, the value of the second car that your parents held onto would have also increased dramatically. Thus, your family would indirectly benefit from the increased value of GM cars, although they still had not sold the second car. This would be much like GM's value in the view of investors also increasing dramatically, and thereby benefitting everyone who owns its stock.

There are two major U.S. exchanges where brokers actually buy and sell shares of public companies in the secondary market for their clients: the New York Stock Exchange and the National Association of Securities Dealers Automated Quote System. We will discuss these exchanges further in Chapter 8.

> For more information, website links, videos, and any assignments associated with this chapter, please visit:
>
> www.teenvestor.com/chapter3

TeenVestor

4

BALANCE SHEET BASICS

If a stranger asks you to invest in his business, the first question you should ask yourself is: how do I know I will get my money back? To answer this question, you would want to know the type of business this individual runs, what equipment his company owns to make his product or deliver his service, how much money he has borrowed from other people, and how much of his own money he has already invested in the business. The answers to these questions will determine whether you feel comfortable parting with your hard-earned money for this investment. A *balance sheet* will give you some of those answers.

THE PIECES OF A BALANCE SHEET

A balance sheet is a snapshot of what a company owns (assets), what it owes (*liabilities*), and the amount of money the owners have invested in the company (*shareholder's equity*, *owner's equity* or just plain *equity*). One thing that is always true about balance sheets is that assets are equal to the sum of liabilities and shareholder's equity. In other words, the formula below must always hold true:

Assets = Liabilities + Equity

This always holds true because what a company owns (its assets) are purchased by the money the company either borrowed (liabilities) or has acquired through the contributions of the partners (shareholder's equity).

The balance sheet is produced based on an idea developed more than 500 years ago called "double-entry accounting" by an Italian mathematician named Luca Pacioli. Double-entry accounting provides an easy way for businesses to keep track of their assets, liabilities, and shareholder's equity.

To illustrate how such a system works, let's use the SportsTee example from the previous chapter. Recall that initially the company collected $3,500 in cash because the 5 partners each contributed $500 of their own money and also borrowed a total of $1,000 from their parents. If SportsTee uses $680 of that money to buy equipment, it has to record (on paper or in a computer spreadsheet) the transaction this way:

Cash went down by $680 ($2820 remains in bank)
The value of equipment went up by $680

As you can see, the business can trace exactly what happened to its money by showing what items increased in value and what items decreased in value. Notice that the purchase of the equipment forced SportsTee to make two entries in a book where it keeps its records. One entry shows that it pulled cash out of its bank account, and another shows that the balance of the equipment it owns went up by the same amount. This method of keeping track of a company's activity is called double-entry accounting because at least two types of *accounts* (categories of assets, liabilities, and equity) are always affected. Things can get more complicated than this, but we hope you understand the basic idea.

Balance sheets have dates attached to them because assets, liabilities and shareholder's equity can change every day. So when you see a balance sheet, you will probably also see the date it was created on the top of the table.

Let's go back to our SportsTee example to understand balance sheets. Given SportsTee's initial investment, a balance sheet that shows the company's assets, liabilities and shareholder's equity can be put together.

Table 4.1 shows SportsTee's balance sheet on its first day of operation. This balance sheet was created using the balances from Table 3.1 in the previous chapter, which shows the total amount the partners need to open up the business.

On Table 4.1, SportsTee's assets are broken down into two sections: *Current Assets* and *Property, Plant & Equipment (Fixed Assets)*. The current assets consist of: cash set aside for advertising, cash set aside to pay workers, cash set aside for rent, cash set aside for miscellaneous purchases, and the value of the inventory (i.e., raw T-shirts). The total current asset balance is $2,820.

TABLE 4.1	
SportsTee's Initial Balance Sheet	
(On Its First Day of Operation)	
Current Assets	
Cash, Inventory (Raw Shirts)	$ 2,820
Property, Plant, & Equipment (Fixed Assets)	
Brushes, Paints, Overalls, Bucket	$680
Total Assets	**$3,500**
Liabilities	
Short-Term Debt (Or Current Liabilities) &	$600
Long-Term Debt	$400
Equity (Including Retained Earnings)	$2,500
Total Liabilities + Equity	**$3,500**

Property, plant and equipment on the balance sheet consist of paint, brushes, buckets, and overalls. It totals $680. The total asset balance is $3,500.

SportsTee was able to buy these assets because of the $3,500 acquired by using the $2,500 contributed by the partners (the equity) and the $1,000 they borrowed (the liability). Therefore, the liability and equity balance is $3,500. When you think about it, this makes perfect sense because all assets owned by SportsTee were acquired by using the money its owners borrowed or contributed. It is worth repeating that this fundamental accounting concept can be represented by the following mathematical formula:

Assets = Liabilities (borrowed money) + Equity (contributed money)

THE TYPICAL CORPORATE BALANCE SHEET

In all balance sheets, you will find the asset, liability and shareholder's equity categories. However, when you start to look at balance sheets for companies in different businesses, you will see big differences in the details of what makes up assets and liabilities. For example, the assets of a car manufacturer like Ford Motor Company will include the big equipment the company uses to make cars. But how about a company that doesn't really manufacture anything – say, an accounting firm such as KPMG? Unfortunately, the double-entry accounting method does not have a good way to record knowledge as an asset on the balance sheet. For this reason, we will concentrate on the balance sheets of manufacturing companies to illustrate the typical corporate balance sheet. As you start getting interested in industries that offer information and business know-how, you can learn about the structure of their balance sheets. This chapter is just to give you a taste of some of the ways information is presented to you about companies, and how you can use the information to help you determine whether you should invest or not.

The balance sheets for most big manufacturing companies will look a little different from SportsTee's balance sheet. For one thing, the asset, liability and equity balances for big companies are much larger. The most recent asset, liability and equity figures from an annual statement (rounded to the nearest million) for Ford are as follows:

Assets:	$224.93 billion
Liabilities:	$196.19 billion
Equity:	$28.74 billion

Another reason why the balance sheet of most big companies will look different from SportsTee's is that these companies have been in business for a long time, so there are categories of assets and liabilities that reflect this fact.

Table 4.2 shows the categories in which many manufacturing companies place their assets, liabilities, and equity. The assets in this typical balance sheet are broken out into current assets and fixed assets.

Current Assets on the Corporate Balance Sheet

This balance sheet shows that current assets are made up of: cash in bank accounts; marketable securities – that is, certificates of deposit (CDs), U.S. Treasury Bills and Notes, and others items that can easily be converted to cash; *accounts receivable* – the amount of money owed to the company for goods sold or services delivered; and inventory – the value of finished, unsold products and raw materials.

Fixed Assets on the Corporate Balance Sheet

Fixed assets are made up of: property, plant, and equipment (less depreciation) – that is, buildings, machines, and land used by the company to make its products (see an explanation of depreciation later in this chapter); prepaid expenses – bills the company pays ahead of time such as rent; patents and goodwill; and marketable securities – long-term certificates of deposit (CDs), long-term U.S. Treasury Bills and Notes, and other items that mature in over one year.

```
┌─────────────────────────────────────────────────────────┐
│                        TABLE 4.2                          │
│         The Typical Corporate Balance Sheet Items         │
│               (For Manufacturing Companies)               │
│                                                           │
│  Total Assets                                             │
│  Current Assets                                           │
│          Cash                                             │
│          Marketable Securities                            │
│          Accounts Receivable                              │
│          Inventory                                        │
│  Fixed Assets                                             │
│          Property, Plant, & Equipment (at Cost)           │
│           Less Depreciation                               │
│          Prepaid Expenses                                 │
│          Patents and Goodwill                             │
│                                                           │
│  Liabilities                                              │
│  Total Current Liabilities                                │
│          Accounts Payable                                 │
│          Notes Payable                                    │
│          Accrued Expenses                                 │
│  Total Long-Term Liabilities                              │
│          Long-Term Debt                                   │
│  Equity                                                   │
│          Common Stock                                     │
│          Preferred Stock                                  │
│          Retained Earnings                                │
└─────────────────────────────────────────────────────────┘
```

Current Liabilities on the Corporate Balance Sheet

Table 4.2 breaks down the typical corporate current liabilities into three sections: accounts payable – money the company owes for products or services it has purchased; notes payable – money the company has borrowed for a short period (usually a year or less); and accrued expenses – wages, taxes and other expenses the company has not yet paid but should pay shortly.

Accrued Expenses is worthy of further explanation. This expense item is on the balance sheet because the company will have to pay some expenses every two weeks (wages, for example), every three months (taxes, for example), or every month (rent or leases, for example), but it has to accumulate the cash to pay the expenses before the payment date. For example, if you pay your friend $7 each week, once a week, for a task he helps you do around the house, you will add $1 to accrued expenses on your personal balance sheet each day, until the seventh day when you'd have to pay him. At that time, accrued expenses go back down to zero because you have made the payment. Accrued expenses allow companies to keep track of bills such as wages and other items they pay periodically.

Long-Term Liabilities on the Corporate Balance Sheet

In Table 4.2, the typical corporate long-term liability is simply the money owed by the company due in over one year. Remember that this money has been borrowed from lenders who expect to be paid interest on the loan whether the company does well or not.

Equity and Retained Earnings on the Corporate Balance Sheet

In Table 4.2, the typical corporate equity amount consists of common stock, preferred stock and retained earnings. Recall that common stock and preferred stock are the money put into the company by investors, and retained earnings are the profit kept by the company (and not distributed as dividends). Please note that unlike SportsTee, which initially had 5 investors or shareholders, a company such as Ford had about 4 billion shares outstanding at the time of this writing.

DEPRECIATION

While it isn't necessary now to go through every category of the typical company balance sheet in greater detail, there is at least one category under fixed (or long-term) assets you should be aware of: *depreciation*.

Depreciation is an important concept because it reflects how much of the company's assets have been used up. You may recall from the previous chapter that SportsTee had to buy a high-quality bucket for $120 to create its product. Let's assume the bucket will be worn out in four years, so SportsTee will have to discard it at that time. If SportsTee expects the bucket to be worthless in 4 years, it means that each year, the company will use up a quarter of the bucket's value, or approximately $30 (1/4 x $120). At the end of the first year, then, the value of the bucket used up would be $30. See Table 4.3 for an illustration of depreciation. If SportsTee had a balance sheet for the end of the year, the bucket would be shown as presented on Table 4.3 (under the column labeled "End of Year 1"). That is, the original value of the bucket will be shown, followed by a depreciation amount (which is a negative number), and then the final value of the bucket, reflecting the depreciation.

This reduction in the value of the assets is considered an expense, and it should reduce the income SportsTee reports to the Internal Revenue Service, the tax collector for the U.S. government.

For simplicity, we have ignored the depreciation of SportsTee's assets on its balance sheet.

Depreciation is important for understanding *book value* – the value of the company if it goes bankrupt. Book value will be further discussed in the next chapter. For some investors, it is an important figure to know when trying to determine whether they should invest in a company or not.

TABLE 4.3

SportsTee Depreciation Item on Balance Sheet
(Day 1 Depreciation Compared With Year-End Depreciation)

	Day 1	End of Year 1
Bucket	$120	$120
Depreciation	-$ 0	-$ 30
Net Value	$120	$ 90

For more information, website links, videos, and any assignments associated with this chapter, please visit:

www.teenvestor.com/chapter4

5

WHAT THE BALANCE SHEET REVEALS

The balance sheet can answer three basic questions that should be on every Teenvestor's mind when evaluating a company:

1. Can the company pay its debt?

2. Has the company borrowed too much money?

3. What is the company worth if it goes out of business?

In the next few sections, we will explain how a balance sheet can help you answer these questions.

CAN THE COMPANY PAY THOSE IT OWES MONEY?

There are some tests a beginning investor can easily perform on a company's balance sheet just to see whether that company can pay its bills. The first test checks whether the company has enough money to pay back debt that is due right away. The second test checks whether the balances of specific assets and liabilities are improving or getting worse.

Current Ratio

Whether the company can pay those it owes money, otherwise known as *creditors*, depends on how much cash it can get its hands on when the bills are due. Just think of your personal situation at home. Whether your parents can pay the electricity or phone bill depends on whether they have cash in the bank, whether they can borrow money to pay the bill, or whether they can sell assets (such as a car) to gather enough cash to pay the bill.

Your parents can't really depend on selling their car as a way to pay such bills, because it may take a long time to find a buyer for the car and negotiate the proper sale price. In short, their ability to pay their bills (a bill being a form of current liabilities) depends on their current assets, and not on their fixed or long-term assets, because current assets consist of either cash or assets that can easily be sold to get cash (also called *liquid assets*). To determine whether a company can pay its bills, you have to look at the size of its current assets versus its current liabilities. On the SportsTee balance sheet on Table 5.1, the current asset balance is $2,820, while the current liability balance (which is short-term debt in this case) is $600. With these two numbers, we can calculate the *current ratio* by dividing the current assets by the current liabilities:

Current Ratio = Current Assets / Current Liabilities

Current Ratio = $2,820 / $600 = 4.7

TABLE 5.1	
SportsTee Initial Balance Sheet	
(On Its First Day of Operation)	
Current Assets	
Cash, Inventory (Raw Shirts)	$2,820
Property, Plant, & Equipment	
Brushes, Paints, Overalls, Bucket	$680
Total Assets	**$3,500**
Liabilities	
Short-Term Debt (Or Current Liabilities)	$600
Long-Term Debt	$400
Equity (Includes Retained Earnings)	$2,500
Total Liabilities + Equity	**$3,500**

This ratio indicates that current assets are nearly 5 times the size of current liabilities. The way to interpret this current ratio is that SportsTee has about 5 times as much cash and liquid assets as it needs to pay bills that will soon become due. This figure makes sense only if you compare the current ratios of the same company over a period of time or the current ratios of different companies in the same type of business. The higher the current ratio, the better. A high current ratio does not guarantee that a company is a winner. It is only one of many indicators that can help tell you if the company is worth a second look.

Changes in Asset Balances

You will find that what really matters with a balance sheet is how it changes from year to year (or period to period). From this point of view, we will look at a few major items on a typical company balance sheet to see how the increase or decrease in balances helps or hurts the company.

Cash

Cash is the money the company has on hand or in bank accounts. In general, we consider an increase in cash to be a good thing, because it can indicate that the company can better withstand hard times when things get difficult.

Accounts Receivable

An increase in accounts receivable is not necessarily good news. Recall that accounts receivable indicates the amount of money owed to the company by its customers. A high accounts receivable balance sounds like it might be a good thing until you discover that the company has already claimed that amount as part of its profit.

A good example would be if you sold your bicycle to an unreliable friend for $150, but he has not paid you yet. On your personal balance sheet, you will have an accounts receivable entry for $150. Now, you can brag to your other friends that you sold the bike at a good price, but the fact that you have not yet received the money makes your claim questionable, because you may never receive that money. Most businesses do the same thing you have done with the sale of your bike. They "brag" (by showing the $150 on a statement that indicates how much money they have made) about their sales before actually collecting the money from customers.

You would expect that if a company's sales were growing, then the accounts receivable would also grow. To tell whether accounts receivable are growing too fast, you should compare them with the growth in sales (which we will talk about in the next chapter). Ideally, the growth of accounts receivable should be less than or equal to the growth in sales.

Inventory

Inventory is the finished goods the company sells, or the raw materials it needs to produce them. In the SportsTee example, the inventory is basically the raw T-shirts. Increasing inventory is good only if the company expects to make and sell more items in the near future. For the most part, however, increasing inventory sometimes signals that the company is not selling enough of its products. An increase in inventory is usually a bad sign.

Accounts Payable

In general, an increasing accounts payable balance can be a good thing, because this means that the company is delaying payments to those it owes money. By delaying payments, it is more or less getting a loan at a low rate for a short period of time.

Think of your parents' credit card payments. When your parents use a charge card to make a $100 purchase, they effectively create an accounts payable of $100 on their personal balance sheet. They will have to pay the credit card company $100 when the bill is due. If they choose to, they can send a $100 check to the credit card company the day after making the purchase – before the bill even arrives at your house. But why should they pay the bill so quickly when the credit card company will probably not bill them for the charge until the end of the month? They can probably use that $100 for their immediate needs and wait for the bill to come. In this way, they are effectively getting an interest-free loan from the credit card company for the number of days it will take the bill to reach your house.

An increase in accounts payable due to the fact that the company can't pay its bills could mean trouble. But this trouble may show up in your current ratio calculation anyway. For a relatively stable company, rising accounts payable is a good thing.

HAS THE COMPANY BORROWED TOO MUCH?

The next important question that the balance sheet can answer is whether the company has borrowed too much money. On a personal level, you probably know that it is not good to owe lots of money. For one thing, the bigger your debt, the more of your allowance or salary you would have to use to pay people back. Of course this means you would have less money to spend on the things that you need to live day to day.

Many investors also look at the amount of debt owed by companies to determine whether these companies are good long-term investments. Typically, investors consider the *debt-equity ratio*, which is simply long-term debt divided by equity (including preferred stock, common stock and retained earnings). SportsTee's debt-equity ratio is 0.16 ($400/$2,500). Hewlett-Packard Company and General

Motors Corporation had debt-equity ratios of 0.10 and 6.28, respectively, at the time of this writing. As you can see from these numbers, different industries have different standards of how much debt is normal. The computer and electronics business typically has much smaller debt-equity ratios than the automobile business. Therefore, it is important to compare the debt levels of companies in the same industries. In general, however, all things being equal, less debt is better than more debt.

We recommend that beginning investors look for companies that have debt-equity ratios less than or equal to 0.50. If a Teenvestor is interested in an industry that has traditionally high debt-equity ratios, she should choose companies with the lowest debt-equity ratios in that industry. In addition, it is best to calculate a debt-equity ratio over several years to see whether it is increasing or decreasing. It is usually good when debt-equity ratios are going down over time. You will find more information about debt-equity ratios in Chapter 13.

WHAT IS THE COMPANY WORTH IF IT GOES BANKRUPT?

The balance sheet can also tell you the value of the company if it were to go bankrupt. This "value" is called *book value* and it can be illustrated with SportsTee. Book value represents the difference between the assets and liabilities on the balance sheet:

Book Value = Assets – Liabilities

It represents what the company is worth when it sells all its assets and pays off all its liabilities. (Note that this is also equal to Equity). Using the balance sheet on Table 3, Book Value = $3,500 - $1,000 = $2,500. The *book value per share* is the book value divided by the number of shares outstanding. SportsTee's book value per share is $500 ($2,500 book value/5 shares). Book value per share differs from *market value per share* in one very important respect: market value per share is the price you will find in the newspapers or on financial websites for a particular stock. Book value per share is simply based on the value of the company here and now if it went out of business.

The way investors typically use book value per share is to compare it with market value per share. They reason that if a company's book value is more than its market value, this could be an indication that the stock is underpriced, and its value may eventually go up if the market's view of the company's market value is wrong. In general, book value gives some indication of the financial health of manufacturing companies with significant fixed assets. The problems with book values and balance sheets in general are explored in the next section.

WHAT THE BALANCE SHEET CANNOT REVEAL

The balance sheet is only one of the items investors look at when evaluating a company to see whether its stock is a good investment. It is probably not the most important tool for looking at all companies. It is fine for looking at some companies that manufacture things, but not necessarily for looking at companies that provide information, because these companies' assets are primarily the "brain power" or the know-how they offer their customers. For example, the main assets of newspapers and magazines are the writers who use their intellectual skills to craft good articles. In addition, some Internet companies that offer their technological know-how can't be evaluated simply by looking at their balance sheets.

One example of how balance sheet analysis can break down is with book value. We believe investors put too much faith in book value as an indicator of a bargain. One shortcoming of book value is that assets on the balance sheet do not include intangible assets such as intellectual capacity (the know-how) and the value of a brand name. For example, the most important asset of a company that writes and produces software is its people – those who use the various computer languages to come up with innovative software packages. There is no way to properly value people when they produce items such as software. Another example where the tangible assets of the company may not necessarily reflect the true value of its assets is the McDonald's Corporation. Any company can sell hamburgers, but if a company can get golden arches and a McDonald's sign in front of its store (with permission from McDonald's, of course), people looking for a quick meal will immediately know what to expect if they stop there. The value of the McDonald's name is not reflected in the tally of its assets when calculating its book value.

Even for companies whose assets are primarily tangible, there is one major shortcoming: book value can be misleading because the value of an asset you see on many balance sheets is not the true value you would get for those assets if you wanted to sell them today. The value of the assets on a balance sheet is called *historical value*, while the true value of an asset is called *market value*. Suppose, for example, that under Property, Plant, and Equipment on the SportsTee balance sheet on Table 5.1 the current or market value was really $280 instead of $680 as shown. This would have made the total asset balance $3,100, not $3,500. The total book value would have been $2,100 ($3,100 in assets less $1,000 in liabilities), and therefore the book value per share would have been $420 per share, not $500 per share as previously calculated. You can see that when the value of Property, Plant, and Equipment is adjusted from $680 to $280, the book value goes down by $80 per share.

Note that depreciation plays a prominent role in a company's book value. Since depreciation reduces the value of the fixed assets on the balance sheet, it tends to reduce book value. But what if a company applies less depreciation than it should on the fixed assets? For example, SportsTee could theoretically show the bucket with its original value of $120 on the balance sheet after one year, even though, as we saw in the previous section, the depreciation of the bucket reduces its value to $90 in that period. By proper depreciation not being applied, the book value of SportsTee would be calculated as $30 higher than it should be.

All this is to say that book value can vary depending on how the assets on the balance sheet are valued. Therefore, it is not always a reliable measure of the company's value if it breaks up.

For more information, website links, videos, and any assignments associated with this chapter, please visit:
www.teenvestor.com/chapter5

6

INCOME STATEMENT BASICS

An *income statement* shows the amount of money a company takes in, the company's expenses, and the *net earnings* (also known as *net profit*, *net income*, or just plain *earnings*) of the company over a specific period. The net income or net earnings is the amount of money the company has left after paying its expenses and its taxes. Table 6.1 shows SportsTee's income statement for one year. The company's net earnings were based on the number and sales price of shirts sold during the year, the cost of the shirts, the other expenses associated with the business, and the taxes paid by the company. We will describe each of these components in detail. Follow the numbers on the side of the income statement.

TABLE 6.1
SportsTee's Income Statement
(At The End Of The First Year Of Operation)

1.	Number of Shirts Sold	1,200
2.	Sales Price of Each Shirt	$15
3.	Total Revenue (#1 Times #2)	$18,000
4.	Total Cost of Raw (Unpainted) Shirts	($3,600)
5.	Cost of Paint & Brushes & Overalls	($2,650)
6.	Depreciation of Bucket	($30)
7.	Rental of Space Per Year	($1,200)
8.	Advertising	($600)
9.	Total Labor by All 5 Owners	($7,200)
10.	Interest on Loan (10% On loan)	($100)
11.	Total Expenses (Sum of #4 to #10)	($15,380)
12.	Earnings Before Taxes (#3 Less #11)	$2,620
13.	Tax (#12 Times 40%)	$1,048
14.	**Net Earnings (#12 Less #13)**	**$1,572**

The line numbers below describe some components of Table 6.1:

#1 *Shirts Sold* – the number of shirts sold by Susan and her four partners during the year. Here, Susan and her friends sold 1,200 shirts.

#2 *Sales Price* – the sale price for each shirt. Here, each shirt is sold for $15.

#3 *Revenue* (also known as Sales) – the amount of money taken in by a company when it sells its goods. In this case, Total Revenue is the product of the total number of shirts sold and the sale price for each shirt: (1,200 shirts) x ($15 per shirt) = $18,000.

#11 *Total Expenses* – This is the sum of the expense items for SportsTee (items #4 to #10). Pay particular attention to the depreciation and the interest rate figures (# 6 and #10). Because we assume the bucket will wear out in four years, we have to recognize as an expense the portion of the bucket that is used up each year – in other words, one-quarter of the bucket's original value, or $30. The interest is the amount of interest that has to be paid on the money borrowed to start the business.

#12 to #14 *Earnings Before Taxes* (#12) is the amount of money the company takes in less the expenses of the company. #13 is the amount of taxes the company pays on the Earnings Before Taxes. #14 is the *Net Earnings* (or *Net Income* or *Net Profit*) – what is left after paying everything you owe, including taxes.

There are really three main components of the income statement: Total Revenue (line #3), Total Expenses (line #11), and Net Earnings (line #14). In general, investors look at the growth of Net Earnings as it relates to the amount of shares in the company.

Corporations usually release their earnings for each three-month interval during their *fiscal year*. These are called *quarterly earnings*. A fiscal year is the one-year period in which the company measures its performance. This period can be from January 1 to

December 31 or any other one-year period such as from February 1 to January 31. In fact, a company can define its fiscal year as beginning in any month and ending 12 months later. A company that has its fiscal year beginning on January 1 will release quarterly earnings for the following periods: January 1 to March 31, April 1 to June 30, July 1 to September 30, and October 1 to December 31. On the other hand, a company with a fiscal year that begins on February 1 will release quarterly earnings for the following periods: February 1 to April 30, May 1 to July 31, August 1 to October 30, and November 1 to January 31.

Stock analysts compare earnings from one quarter to the corresponding previous year's quarter. This type of comparison is reasonable because some businesses are seasonal. That is, sales in some quarters are bigger than in others. In the case of SportsTee, Susan and her friends may find that their T-shirts are more popular in May, when it starts to warm up in the Northeast, than in January, when it is cold. It makes sense for SportsTee to compare sales in the current period with the same period in a previous year. This practice is even more justified with retail stores, because many of them make 30% to 40% of their year's sales during the Christmas holiday season. It makes perfect sense for these stores to compare sales of one Christmas season with the previous Christmas season.

> For more information, website links, videos, and any assignments associated with this chapter, please visit:
>
> www.teenvestor.com/chapter6

7

WHAT THE INCOME STATEMENT REVEALS

The income statement can reveal a lot of information that investors can use to make decisions on what stocks to buy. In this chapter, we will show you how to use some of this information to understand a company's profitability.

EARNINGS PER SHARE

One very important figure most investors look at is how much profit each shareholder makes for each dollar he or she invests. This is usually called *earnings per share*, and it is calculated by dividing after-tax earnings by the number of shares issued by the company. For the SportsTee example, this can be calculated by dividing its net earnings, $1,572 (as calculated in the previous chapter) by the 5 shares held by Susan and her partners. This calculation, $1,572/5, is equal to $314.40 earned per share. The latest available full-year earnings per share for International Business Machines Corporation (IBM) and McDonald's Corporation at the time of this writing were $4.12 and $1.40, respectively. These companies have smaller earnings-per-share figures than SportsTee because such giant corporations have a lot of shares *outstanding* – that is, shares in the hands of investors. As we mentioned in a previous chapter, Ford Motor Company, for example, has about 4 billion shares outstanding.

Earnings per share, or EPS as it's commonly called, is more meaningful when you look at EPS growth from period to period and when you compare it with the EPS of other companies in the same line of business. We will discuss EPS in full in Chapter 13.

NET PROFIT MARGIN

In addition to EPS, another way to measure how profitable a company was in any given year is through its *net profit margin* (also known as profit margin). Net profit margin is a company's net earnings divided by its total revenue. For SportsTee, the revenue was $18,000 and the net earnings were $1,572, so the calculation of net profit margin (in percentage terms) is as follows:

Net Profit Margin = $1,572 x 100 / 18,000 = 8.7%

What this means is that SportsTee kept only 8.7% of the revenue it took in during the year. This number is useful only when you compare it with the net profit margin of the same company in prior years, or when you compare it with the net profit margin of other companies in the same business as SportsTee.

Big corporations also have tiny net profit margins. This is always a big surprise to Teenvestors who, like most people, think that companies keep a lot more money than they do. Ford Motor Company, for example, had a net profit margin of 2.4% at the time of this writing. This meant that out of revenue of $144.1 billion, it kept about $3.4 billion – a big sum of money, but not so big when you compare it with the company's revenue.

DIVIDENDS AND RETAINED EARNINGS

After a company determines how much money it has made during the year, it has to decide what to do with that money. It can do basically two things: pay it to its shareholders or plow it back into the company to buy equipment or expand the business. The biggest companies in America, such as IBM and McDonald's, often pay some of the profits to shareholders as *dividends* and also keep some of the money in the company. The money kept in the company is called *retained earnings*, and you will find it under the equity section of the balance sheet. You can think of retained earnings as additional equity that the owners of the company have contributed to the business.

Many fast-growing companies do not pay dividends because they would rather plow their earnings back into the company to maintain their technological dominance or get more stability in earnings. For example, Apple began paying regular dividends to its stockholders in 2012. *USA Today* said this of Apple's move at that time:

The dividend ushers in a new era for Apple, where the company financially transitions from being a scrappy upstart that pours its profit into new products, into more of a mature firm that generates more cash than it can use.... And the move makes Apple less of a speculative play and more of a candidate for investors looking for a mature company. The dividend is a steady payment of cash for investors who have become accustomed to collecting on the stock's breathtaking capital gains... The dividend signals a significant financial shift for Apple, as the company's cash generation from profitability far outstrips its internal needs for expansion, research and hiring.

Table 7.1 shows that even though SportsTee made $1,572 after taxes during the year, it distributed only $1,000 to the five Teenvestors that own the business. Therefore, each partner actually received $200 ($200 = $1,000 / 5). The remaining $572 was put back into the company, and it can be viewed as the additional money the five investors put into the company above and beyond their original investment of $500 each.

TABLE 7.1		
Effect of Paying Dividends		
(Retained Earnings)		
Earnings Before Taxes	=	$2,620
Net Earnings (After Paying 40% Tax On Earnings)	=	$1,572
Net Earnings Paid As Dividends	=	($1,000)
Net Earnings Retained In Company	=	**$572**

The $572 figure, which represents retained earnings, is added to the original equity investment of $2500 ($500 per partner x 5 =

$2,500) for a total equity balance of $3,072. The lesson here is that profits not distributed as dividends represent additional investments by the shareholders.

THE DIVIDEND YIELD

The *dividend yield*, the ratio of the dividend per share to the price of each share, is another frequently watched figure in the stock-picking game. The dividend per share for each SportsTee stockholder is $200 ($200 = $1,000 / 5 shareholders). Therefore, the dividend yield is 40% ($200/$500), since the dividend per share is $200 and the price of each share owned by the SportsTee partners is $500.

Most companies pay out a fixed dollar amount of dividends per share from year to year, with occasional adjustments. For many investors, dividend yield is important because it provides them with a steady source of income above any possible increase in the value of the stock. But when you think about it, a high dividend yield could mean that the share price has gone down, which could mean a loss to you when it is time to sell. Buying stock based on dividend yield can also be faulty because companies that are not doing well can easily cut or eliminate their dividends. The lesson here is that dividend yields can vary greatly because they depend on share prices and the economic conditions that companies are facing.

The stocks of stable, well-established companies that have paid dividends to investors over a long time, and that are no longer growing at a fast pace, are known as *blue-chip stocks*. When Teenvestors begin investing, they should start with shares in these types of companies. However, as they gain more experience as investors, we also recommend that they gradually buy shares in faster growing companies that may not pay dividends but instead, plow all their profits back into the company to help it thrive. The stocks of these types of companies are known as *growth stocks*. To illustrate why growth stocks can be desirable, take another look at SportsTee. Recall that the company paid $1,000 in dividends to the five shareholders. If you were looking at investing in SportsTee, wouldn't you prefer to see that the company is plowing back all its earnings into the company to buy new equipment, do more advertising, and spend money trying to nurture the company? We would, because we know that the company is laying the groundwork to do really well in the future. This is how Teenvestors should be thinking. They should seek to hold in their *portfolios* (their bags of investments) some shares of these types of growth-oriented stocks. But a majority of their shares should remain blue-chip stocks until they become super-advanced investors.

For more information, website links, videos, and any assignments associated with this chapter, please visit:

www.teenvestor.com/chapter7

8

UNDERSTANDING THE MARKET

The Market. You hear and see the term in the financial news every day. Your parents may even talk about it. But do you know what it really means?

Without getting into a precise definition, the phrase "the market" usually refers to the stock market. When people ask about the condition of the market, they are asking whether prices of stocks are generally increasing or decreasing.

Knowing that the market exists is one thing, but knowing how to measure the health of the market is another. In the U.S. economy, experts have come up with ways to measure the market. In this chapter, we will discuss the marketplace where stocks are bought and sold, and the various measures that investors use to tell how the market is doing.

WHERE STOCK IS BOUGHT AND SOLD

Stockbrokers trade (in other words, buy and sell) stock through *exchanges* – institutions such as the New York Stock Exchange (NYSE) and the National Association of Securities Dealers Automated Quotation System (NASDAQ). Each of these exchanges has its own rules and regulations that govern which companies can be listed on them.

Launched in 1817, the NYSE lists some of the biggest companies in the United States. The American Stock Exchange, which was launched in 1842 and was commonly viewed as the younger sibling of the NYSE, merged with the NYSE in 2008. NASDAQ was started in 1971 as the exchange for smaller companies, but it has grown to include some of the biggest technology companies in the United States.

You don't have to know whether a stock is traded on the NYSE or NASDAQ when you buy or sell shares. Your stockbroker or your online broker will simply buy the shares for you – they are the ones who have to know where to go.

At the end of each day, these exchanges record what is known as *closing prices* for each stock. Closing prices are generally the last price during the day at which the stock was bought or sold. The closing prices in these exchanges are often used to tell how the stock market is doing.

STOCK MARKET INDICATORS YOU SHOULD KNOW

An indicator is a number that gives you an idea of the qualities that you are trying to measure. For example, let's say that you want an easy way to gauge how the temperature in your town changes from day to day without having to measure the temperature yourself. One way to do this is to find out the temperature in, say, 10 locations around the boundary of your county and divide by ten. This average would probably be a good approximation of the temperature in your town. Obviously, to get a more precise number, you would have to measure the temperature in a lot more than 10 locations in your county. The average temperature of these 10 spots is now your indicator or *index* for your town's temperature. You can call it anything you want: The Teenvestor Temperature Index, The TTI, or whatever you like. If this index is calculated and published every day by some organization, you can get an approximation on how the temperature in your town changes by looking at the changes in the index alone.

The following are the three important stock market indicators or indexes most stock experts use to tell how stocks are doing: the Dow Jones Industrial Average (the Dow or the DJIA), the Standard & Poor's 500 (the S&P 500), and the NASDAQ Composite Index (the NASDAQ Composite).

The Dow Jones Industrial Average

The most prominent stock market indicator in the United States is the Dow. Charles Henry Dow first published the Dow on May 26, 1896. At that time, it included the sum of the prices of just 12 so-called "smoke stack" companies, such as coal and gas companies. Today, the Dow is made up of 30 stocks of some of the biggest companies in America. Table 8.1 lists the companies that are included in the Dow. The stocks for the Dow are pulled primarily from the NYSE. Of the original 12 stocks included in the Dow, General Electric is the only company still on the list.

The index is calculated by summing up the "adjusted prices" of the stocks of the companies listed on the table. The adjusted prices are the stock price for each company, adjusted for things such as *stock splits* (further explained on our website). You won't be able to calculate the Dow on your own by averaging all the closing prices of the 30 stocks that make it up, without knowing how to adjust the price of each stock. But Teenvestors shouldn't really care about how the Dow is calculated. All that should matter to them is whether the index goes up or down, and by how much.

When you hear or read that the Dow went up 20 points, you can think of it as meaning that the average of the stock prices in the Dow went up by $20. Sometimes the change in the Dow is given in percentage terms such as "The Dow was up 15% yesterday." As long as you know in what terms the change is expressed – whether in points or in percentage – you can gauge the seriousness of the change in the Dow.

Many investors focus on the day-to-day changes in the Dow. As a Teenvestor, you shouldn't be concerned with daily changes because you are a long-term investor. You are in stocks for the long haul – four, five, seven years and beyond. As long as you've done your research on a company and feel good about its long-term prospects, declines or increases in the Dow should not get you overly excited.

COMPANY	STOCK SYMBOL
TABLE 8.1	
The 30 Companies in the Dow Jones Industrial Average	
COMPANY	STOCK SYMBOL
Apple Inc.	AAPL
American Express Company	AXP
The Boeing Company	BA
Caterpillar, Inc.	CAT
Chevron Corporation	CVX
Cisco Systems, Inc.	CSCO
The Coca-Cola Company	KO
DuPont (E.I.) de Nemours & Co.	DD
Exxon Mobil Corporation	XOM
General Electric Company	GE
The Goldman Sachs Group, Inc.	GS
The Home Depot, Inc.	HD
Intel Corporation	INTC
International Business Machines Corporation	IBL
JP Morgan Chase & Co.	JPM
Johnson & Johnson	JNJ
McDonald's Corp.	MCD
Merck & Co. Inc.	MRK
Microsoft Corporation	MSFT
Minnesota Mining & Mfg. (3M)	MMM
The Procter & Gamble Company	PG
Nike, Inc.	NKE
Pfizer, Inc.	PFE
The Travelers Companies, Inc.	TRV
UnitedHealth Group Incorporated	UNH
United Technologies Corporation	UTX
Verizon Communications, Inc.	VZ
Visa Inc.	V
Wal-Mart Stores, Inc.	WMT
The Walt Disney Company	DIS

The Dow has been criticized because it measures how big companies are doing and because it does not include some of the types of businesses that now play a role in the economic life of the country. For example, an Internet company like Amazon is currently not on the Dow. What this means is that the Dow does not look much like the portfolio of stocks held by many small investors – especially those investors who like high-technology growth stocks.

To partially respond to this criticism, companies such as Microsoft Corp., Intel Corp., Home Depot and Apple have been added to the Dow, displacing some of the older companies such as Goodyear Tire & Rubber, Union Carbide and others. The Dow remains the oldest and most quoted index of the American stock market.

You will find updates to the Dow and its year-end levels over the past 10 years at www.teenvestor.com/chapter8.

The S&P 500

Another gauge investors use to tell how the market is doing is the Standard & Poor's 500. As the name suggests, there are 500 stocks in this index. These stocks are too numerous to list here, but they include many of the stocks found in the Dow, and they are all among the most widely traded stocks in the United States. The stocks in the S&P 500 are traded on the NYSE and the NASDAQ exchanges. Since the S&P 500 has more stocks in it and covers many more types of businesses than the Dow, it is considered a better measure of how the stock market is doing. Unlike the Dow, which simply sums adjusted stock prices of the 30 stocks it tracks, the S&P

500 is weighted by the size (gauged by market capitalization) of companies in the index. The size weighting involved in producing the S&P 500 index is generally considered by some to produce a better indication of overall stock price movements than an unweighted stock index such as the Dow.

As with the Dow, the change in the S&P 500 is at times given in terms of points (dollar amounts) and at times in terms of percentage.

You will find updates to the S&P 500 and its year-end levels over the past 10 years at www.teenvestor.com/chapter8.

The NASDAQ Composite

The NASDAQ Composite Index (the NASDAQ) is made up of the thousands of stocks traded on the NASDAQ exchange.

Recall that in an earlier section we told you the NASDAQ Exchange is generally where the stocks of smaller, lesser known companies are traded. For this reason, the NASDAQ Composite Index is used to tell how smaller companies are doing. Of late, the NASDAQ Composite has been doing well because of small, high-technology companies that have had huge run-ups in their stock prices.

Like the Dow, the change in the NASDAQ Composite is given in terms of points (dollar amounts) and percentage.

You will find updates to the NASDAQ Composite and its year-end levels over the past 10 years at www.teenvestor.com/chapter8.

How the Dow, the S&P 500, and the NASDAQ Composite Are Related

As you can imagine, there is a relationship among the Dow, the S&P 500, and the NASDAQ Composite, since they are all supposed to give an indication of what is happening in the stock market. In general, when one moves up, the others move up as well especially when there is a major world-wide political, social, or financial event. For example, on June 23, 2016, British citizens went to the polls and voted to withdraw from the European Union. The next day, the stock market plunged as described in the following passage from a *Forbes* article:

> U.S. stocks started the day in the red following the carnage in international markets, with major stock averages each plummeting over 3% during the session. At the close, the Dow Jones Industrial Average had plunged 611 points, or 3.3%, and the S&P 500 lost 3.6%, erasing their 2016 gains. Meanwhile, the Nasdaq fell 4.1%, putting it in correction territory.

The point increase or percentage increase may be different, however, because of the types of stocks included in the various indexes. Because the Dow includes the stocks of the biggest companies in the country, it tends not to move up or down as much as the S&P 500 and the NASDAQ Composite. Just think of the Dow as a big ship that is hard to slow down or speed up.

Even though in general the three indexes move up and down together, there are times when the NASDAQ Composite is out of step with the Dow and the S&P 500. This happened quite frequently during the tech-stock booms that generally occurred around 2000 and again in 2015. The reason was that the NASDAQ Composite is technology-heavy. The index generally performed very well in these periods, regardless of what was happening to the rest of the stocks in the market.

Other Indexes

There are many more indexes that investors use in determining how the stock market is doing in the United States or internationally. Some investors may put their money in specific segments such as Internet-related, oil-related, or transportation-related businesses, so they need indexes that tell them how those businesses are doing in general. Such indexes *do* exist.

We won't go through all of them here, but when you become a more advanced Teenvestor, you can look them all up if you need them. For now, the three major indexes – the Dow, the S&P 500, and the NASDAQ Composite – are all you need to know if you are primarily interested in tracking the performance of stocks traded on U.S. stock exchanges.

Some other significant indexes for other countries include the following:

- The FTSE 100 (FTSE): Index associated with the 100 top U.K.-regulated companies on the London Stock Exchange.
- The DAX Index associated with 30 of the largest German companies traded on the Frankfurt Stock Exchange.
- The Nikkei 225 Index (the Nikkei): Index associated with stocks traded on the Tokyo Stock Exchange.

- The Hang Seng Index: Index associated with stocks traded on the Hong Kong Stock Exchange.

> For more information, website links, videos, and any assignments associated with this chapter, please visit:
>
> www.teenvestor.com/chapter8

9

GOVERNMENT INFORMATION AND ACTIONS THAT AFFECT THE MARKET

The government publishes lots of information to tell the public how the economy is doing. Some investors use this information as a basis for deciding whether to keep their money in the stock market or move it to other investments they consider safer or more profitable. This chapter discusses how financial information and actions by the U.S. government affect the behavior of investors and the market.

GOVERNMENT INFORMATION

Information about how fast prices are going up, the amount of products American industries make and sell, and how many people have jobs are some of the most important things that affect the stock market. In this section, we will show you how these factors make stock prices go up and down.

Inflation and the Consumer Price Index (CPI)

In general, *inflation* is the extent to which your money today will buy less in the future. You have probably come face-to-face with inflation at some point in your life. For example, you may have noticed that the price of a movie ticket has gone up, or that the cost of your favorite food items has increased. There are many reasons why prices go up:

1. Inflation can be caused because more people want a particular product. For example, on Valentine's Day, roses are more expensive because people want to buy them for their spouses and partners.

2. Inflation can occur when companies raise prices in response to higher costs to make the products they are selling. For example, car prices went up slightly when automobile companies were required by law to include air bags in cars.

3. Inflation can be caused by planned shortages. For example, if the companies that produce the oil used to make gasoline decide to cut back on the amount of oil they ship to customers, this could increase the price of oil, and in turn the price of gasoline.

4. Inflation can be caused by fear of shortages. For example, during a war, certain items such as gasoline may go up in price because people are scared their supplies will be cut off, and so they start to hoard it.

The *Consumer Price Index for All Urban Consumers*, or CPI-U, is one measure of inflation used by the government. The U.S. Labor Department produces the monthly CPI-U, which measures the increase in the price of a given "basket" of goods and services purchased by typical consumers. It covers a large number of items, including food, housing, apparel, transportation, medical care, and entertainment. The CPI-U often is used to increase or adjust payments for rents, wages, alimony, child support and other obligations that may be affected by changes in the cost of living.

A very simplified example of how the CPI-U calculation works is that prices are added together for the typical items people buy, and this sum is compared to the same "basket" of goods a year later. For example, a basket of goods could include things like milk, gas, meat, rent, clothes, and other things essential for everyday life. Adding up the prices of these items one year and adding up the prices a year later can tell you whether prices are moving up or down. The percentage increase in price for these goods will be the rate of inflation. Of course, prices can also go down, too, in which case you've got *deflation*.

Inflation is given in percentage terms based on the changes to CPI-U. For example, one way to calculate the inflation rate in 2015 is to compare the December CPI-U figures in 2014 and 2015. These figures were \$234.812 in December 2014 and \$236.525 in December 2015. You can roughly calculate the point-in-time inflation rate (from December to December) in percentage for 2015 as follows:

(CPI-U in 2015 - CPI-U in 2014) × 100 / (CPI-U in 2014) =

(\$236.525 - \$234.812) × 100 / \$234.812 = 0.73%

You can also calculate the average inflation in 2015 by using the average CPI-U in 2014 and 2015 in the formula above. The average CPI-U figures in 2014 and 2015 were $232.957 and $236.736, respectively. You can roughly calculate the average inflation rate in percentage for 2014 as follows:

$$(CPI\text{-}U \text{ in } 2015 - CPI\text{-}U \text{ in } 2014) \times 100 / (CPI\text{-}U \text{ in } 2014) =$$
$$(\$237.017 - \$236.736) \times 100 / \$236.736 = 0.12\%$$

When you see the inflation rate quoted in the media, you have to find out whether the writer or reporter is referring to the average annual inflation rate as calculated in the example above, or a point-in-time inflation rate such as in the prior example. Nevertheless, you can do your own calculation by accessing government CPI-U data through www.teenvestor.com/chapter9. This data consists of CPI-U and inflation rate information going back to 1913. At the time of this writing, the highest average annual inflation rate based on the CPI-U was 17.80% in 1917, and the lowest was negative 10.85% in 1921.

A very low inflation rate may actually indicate that the economy is not doing very well. For example, in 2009, after the worst financial crisis the United States has faced since the Great Depression, the average inflation rate was -0.34%. This was a sharp decline from the 2008 average inflation rate of about 3.85%. Such a steep decline generally indicates that the economy is in deep trouble. One way the government tries to maintain healthy rates of inflation and economic growth is to change an interest rate called the discount rate to affect how much money people borrow and spend. A 2015 article by *The Boston*

Globe, written when the Federal Reserve Bank was contemplating whether to raise interest rates, explains the negative side of low inflation as follows:

> The idea that inflation can be too low is difficult for many people to get their heads around, particularly older Americans, who have watched the Fed fight rising inflation for most of their lives. But some inflation — the Fed says about 2 percent a year — is the sign of a healthy economy, translating into rising wages, appreciating assets, and stronger growth, as well as higher prices. But inflation at the consumer level has been nonexistent in recent months; in July it rose at annual rate of just 0.2 percent, according to the Labor Department. Other economic conditions, including a weakening global economy and falling crude oil prices, suggest inflation will remain low for a while.

To understand how inflation affects the stock market, you first have to understand what determines stock prices of the companies traded on the various exchanges we discussed earlier. The stock price of a company depends on how much that company is expected to make in the future. To make it perfectly clear, net earnings (also known as net income and net profit) drive a company's stock price. In other words, the more you expect a company to earn in the future, the higher the value of the company's stock.

If inflation is high, a company's earnings in the future are worth less and less. That's because what the company earns in the future won't buy the same things it can buy today. If a company's expected earnings are worth less in the future, then its stock price will go down. Therefore, in general, the higher the inflation, the worse things are for the stock market. The relationship between stock prices and inflation is further explained in Chapter 10.

To show you a real example of how the inflation rate (as reflected in the consumer price index) affects the stock market, here is an excerpt from a 2000 article in *The Wall Street Journal*:

> Stocks plunged, with the major indexes enduring their biggest point drops ever and among their steepest percentage losses in a decade. Friday's *consumer-price* report indicated that inflation was resurfacing. The Nasdaq Composite Index dropped 355.49 points, or 9.7%, to 3321.29. The Dow Jones industrials sank 617.78 points to 10,305.77.

This passage above was referring to one of the biggest-ever point drops in the market – for both the Dow and the NASDAQ – which occurred on Friday, April 14, 2000. This drop was caused primarily by a consumer price index report, which showed that inflation jumped by 0.7%.

Inflation also affects the *interest rate* – what you pay to borrow money. The higher the inflation rate, the higher the interest rate. This is because lenders want to make up for the fact that the higher inflation will make the interest borrowers pay to them worth less and less. So, to make up for these losses, they have to increase the amount of interest they charge.

Gross Domestic Product

Gross Domestic Product (GDP) is the dollar value of what the national economy produced during a certain period. You can think of it as the report card for the United States. The GDP includes the following items:

1. How much you, your family, and other citizens spend on food, clothing, services, and other items.

2. The money businesses spend to buy equipment for their factories, the money families spend to buy homes, and the change in certain items on the balance sheets of companies.

3. The money spent by the government for defense, roads, schools, and other items.

4. The amount of goods and services the United States sells to other countries.

Of all the items listed above, the biggest contributor to the GDP is item 1 – how much you, your family, and other citizens spend on food, clothing, services, and other items.

You will rarely see the actual dollar amount of GDP printed anywhere. What you are likely to see is the percentage of growth in GDP. The growth figure is watched very carefully to check the health of the economy. Since 1930, the real GDP growth has ranged from about negative 13% in (in 1932) to about 19% (in 1942.) Over the 10-year period ending in December 2015, the real GDP growth rate ranged from negative 2.8% (reflecting the after-effects of the 2008 financial crisis) to 2.7%.

A fast-growing GDP can lead to inflation, because this probably means that too many consumers are buying goods and services. (When you have more people with more money trying to buy goods and services, prices tend to go up). When the GDP does not grow but instead declines, this is known as a *recession*. As mentioned earlier, one way the government tries to cure too much inflation or a recession by changing the discount rate to the amount of borrowing and spending. This process is described later in this chapter. You can find an Excel spreadsheet of GDP figures published by the U.S. Bureau of Economic Analysis through our website at www.teenvestor.com/chapter9.

The Employment Report

There are a certain number of people in the United States who have jobs (known as *the employed*) at any particular time. There are also a certain number of people who are actively seeking jobs (known as *the unemployed*. Together, the number of people employed and the number of people unemployed make up the *labor force* or *workforce*. These numbers change from time to time, but in 2015 the number of the U.S civilian labor force was approximately 157,130,000. The *unemployment rate* is the percentage of the labor force that is out of work. In 2015, about 8,296,000 people were out of work, yielding an unemployment rate of about 5.3%. Based on data from the U.S. Bureau of Labor Statistics, the highest and lowest unemployment rates since 1947 were 9.7% in 1982 and 2.9% in 1953.

People who are not employed and are not seeking employment are not counted as part of the workforce. Usually, rising employment and declining unemployment are signs of an improving economy.

Most beginning Teenvestors think that a low unemployment rate is good for the stock market. In their minds, it is wonderful when everyone has a job. They are shocked to discover that when an Employment Report shows that the unemployment rate is lower than expected, the stock market actually goes down under normal circumstances. In other words, the Dow, the S&P 500, and the NASDAQ Composite Index generally decline in value. Likewise, when an Employment Report shows the unemployment rate is higher than expected, the stock market generally improves.

The explanation for the stock market's reaction to the Employment Report is that when the unemployment rate is lower than expected, it means more people are working. If more people are working, it also means that more people are going to be spending money, and contributing to the GDP. When more people are spending money, the stock market is scared of that dreaded "I" word – inflation. Fear of inflation usually causes the stock market to go down.

For young investors, this is hard to accept, because while they want the stock market to do well, they also don't want to rejoice when more people are out of work. The only way Teenvestors can feel better about this is to realize that high inflation can decrease the quality of life for tens of millions of Americans in ways that are not always obvious. For example, an increase in mortgage rates (the interest rates that people pay on money they have borrowed to buy their houses), which is caused by inflation, could cost homeowners a few hundred dollars more a month, could discourage people from buying homes in the first place, or could disqualify people who want to borrow money to buy a home. Skyrocketing heating oil prices could mean that some people may not be able to afford oil to keep warm in their homes during the winter.

THE GOVERNMENT ACTIONS THAT AFFECT THE ECONOMY

If the GDP is growing too fast, it means primarily that consumers are spending a lot of money (because consumer spending makes up the majority of the GDP). As you have already learned, when a lot of people with a lot of money are trying to buy the same goods, this typically results in inflation. (Recall that we discussed how on Valentine's Day, roses are more expensive because more people want roses on that day). Things in general become more expensive when too many consumers have money (either money from their jobs or money they have borrowed) to buy these items.

To stop consumers and others who contribute to the GDP from spending too much money too fast, the government (specifically, the Federal Reserve Bank, often just referred to as the Fed makes it harder for people to borrow money by increasing the *discount rate*. This increase, which is known as "tightening monetary policy," eventually makes it more expensive for consumers and others to borrow money from banks. With less money being borrowed, there is less spending. This eventually reduces consumer spending, reduces the possibility of inflation, and causes the GDP to go down.

If the GDP is not growing at all, it probably means that consumers are not spending much money at all. To encourage people to spend more, the Federal Reserve can decrease the discount rate, which eventually makes it easier for consumers to borrow. This action is known as "loosening monetary policy."

You might be puzzled as to why the Federal Reserve has to interfere in the economy in the first place. The first question you might be asking yourself is why the Federal Reserve will raise rates to stop inflation. The best way to think about the Federal Reserve's action is to think of the economy as a train that is running on a schedule. A train that is going too fast can derail and crash. This is what happens when the economy is too hot because of high inflation. Much like the operator of the train who taps on the brakes to slow the train down, the Federal Reserve raises the discount rate to discourage people from borrowing and spending too much so as to slow down the economy and stop it from derailing.

If the train is going really slow, it will not meet its schedule. Much like the operator who tinkers with the train's engine to increase its speed, the Federal Reserve stimulates the economy by reducing the discount rate to encourage more people to borrow and spend. The following passage from *The Wall Street Journal* (June 9, 2000) summarizes some of the concepts we have been teaching regarding the economy and the Fed's action to keep it stable:

> The Nasdaq Composite Index gained 19% last week following a report that unemployment was rising and that businesses were eliminating jobs. That was bad news for job seekers, but it stirred hopes that the economy is slowing. If it starts seeing results from its yearlong campaign to cool the economy, the Fed might finally stop raising rates. Rising rates have been the main brake on the stock and bond markets.... While a slowing economy would help stocks, economic strength could send stocks down.

The Federal Reserve's actions to keep the economy on an even keel make sense if you pause and give it some real thought. The only problem is that it is very difficult to know how quickly, how hard or how long to apply the brakes on the economy, or how much stimulation is needed to get the economy moving again.

HOW EXPECTATIONS DRIVE THE MARKET

The economy affects the stock market in many ways, and the government produces lots of weekly, monthly and quarterly economic data to track and study it.

As we have just discussed, among the most important indicators are: inflation (the increase and decrease of prices), the gross domestic product or GDP (the sum of goods and services produced in the country), the unemployment rate (the number of people who can't find jobs), and the discount rate (the rate set by the government that eventually affects the interest rates your parents pay to borrow money). These economic indicators are all related in one way or another. The stock market continuously adjusts itself by reassessing the value of stocks based on any new financial information it gets. The stock market also adjusts based on the guesses of financial experts on what the government's economic data and the government's actions will be.

As an example of how these indicators affect the stock market, let's examine the effect of the unemployment rate. If, for example, investors think the unemployment rate for the next month will be 5% and it eventually proves to be 4%, there is a pretty good chance that the S&P 500 will go down. As we discussed earlier, the stock market might go down in this case because a lower unemployment rate could trigger inflation, a result of more people having money to buy more goods and services. However, if the unemployment rate comes in at

5% as expected, a stock market index like the S&P 500 will probably not change much.

Real-life evidence of how expectations affect the market can be found, once again, in our earlier example of how the CPI affected the stock market on April 14, 2000. On that day, as discussed earlier, the Dow and the NASDAQ Composite dropped sharply because the newly released CPI showed a 0.7% increase. The major problem was not that the CPI increased, but that people expected an increase of only 0.5%. Here is how the April 17, 2000 issue of *Investor's Business Daily* reported the drop in the market:

> Investor's got a rude awakening Friday. The consumer price index jumped 0.7% in March, the biggest gain in almost a year, casting already-weak stocks into another freefall. The surge was worse than the 0.5% rise most analysts expected.

As you can see, investors were disappointed that inflation was climbing faster than expected, so they pulled their money out of the stock market. Of course, this helped cause the market to tumble.

For more information, website links, videos, and any assignments associated with this chapter, please visit:

www.teenvestor.com/chapter9

TeenVestor

10

BUSINESS AND FINANCIAL CONCEPTS YOU SHOULD KNOW

You will feel a sense of satisfaction when you can listen to financial news on CNN or on Bloomberg and actually understand what they are talking about. With the concepts we explain in this chapter, you will learn some of the most important ideas all investors should know. After reading this chapter those financial news reporters will have nothing on you. In fact, you will probably know more than they do because many reporters just read the news, without understanding it. You, on the other hand, will have the benefit of knowing how the news affects the market.

Subsequent chapters in this book refer to some of the ideas explored here. We suspect that you will have to come back to this chapter again and again because it covers some of the most important business and financial concepts you will ever encounter.

SUPPLY & DEMAND

The law of *supply and demand* is an important idea in the stock market and in the course of everyday life. The principle of supply and demand states that if too many people want something, the price of that thing (whatever it is) will go up. (We briefly discussed this concept in the previous chapter and referred to increasing prices as inflation). The word "supply" usually refers to the availability of the product in question. The word "demand" usually refers to the desire to have that product. If there is too much supply of a product, that product becomes so common that the maker can't really charge very much for it.

Think of a diamond, which is a very expensive precious stone. One of the reasons diamonds are expensive is that the amount available for sale around the world is tightly controlled by a handful of dealers who create an artificial shortage. Because so many people want diamonds (for their wedding engagements and for other special occasions), and because the supply is kept low, the price of diamonds stays high from year to year.

The prices of stocks also change according to how many shares are available and how much people want them. If more people want to sell a particular stock than to buy it, the price of that stock will fall because the stock market is truly a market with sellers (or those who supply stocks) and buyers (or those who want or demand stock).

THE TWO WAYS STOCKS CAN MAKE MONEY

So what attracts buyers to certain stocks and puts them in high demand? Investors put their money into stocks because they want their money to make money. The two ways stocks make money are through the receipt of dividends, and through *capital appreciation*.

Dividends

Just to refresh your memory, dividends are the portion of a company's earnings that is paid to the investor every three months. Companies happily pay dividends when they make money. However, when profits are down or if these companies start losing money, they can decide to stop paying dividends.

The date a company announces the amount of dividends it will pay to its stockholders is called the *declaration date*. But not everyone who owns the company's stock will get the dividends the next time they are paid. It depends on when the shares were purchased. If an investor buys the shares by a date called the *ex-dividend date*, she will receive the current declared dividends. If she buys them just after the ex-dividend date, she will start receiving dividends in about three months – the next time dividends are declared. The dividend is sent to the investor on a date called the *payment date*.

You may find that financial publishers report the yearly dividend of companies instead of the amount that is paid every quarter. So, a quarterly dividend of 50 cents is reported as a $2.00 dividend, or four times the quarterly dividend.

Capital Appreciation

Besides dividends, the only other way to make money with stocks is through *capital appreciation*, or *capital gains* as it is sometimes known. Capital appreciation is the increase in the price of a stock.

THE RELATIONSHIP BETWEEN STOCKS AND BONDS

Even though this book focuses on stock investing, you should be aware of the relationship between stocks and bonds. Just to refresh your memory, a stock represents a piece of a company owned by an investor, and a bond represents a loan to a company or to a government agency for which the lender receives interest payments.

In general, a company's bond is safer than its stock. By "safer" we mean that you are less likely to lose your money with bonds than with stocks when looking at investing in one company. As we discussed earlier, a riskier investment has the potential to pay you more than a safer investment. This is why the interest rates on some bonds are usually low compared with the amount of money you can make when the value of stocks goes up. Of course, there is no guarantee that the value of the stock will go up at all. But this is part of the risk you take when you invest.

Many investors own both stocks and bonds. Sometimes they will switch their money from stocks to bonds, and other times they will do the reverse. Exactly when they make the switch partially depends on inflation. This is because the interest rates paid on bonds depend on inflation – the higher the inflation rate, the more interest borrowers will have to pay lenders to make up for the fact that inflation will eat up the payments they are making to these lenders. Therefore, the higher the interest rates, the more attractive bonds are to most investors looking for a safer place to put their money. This movement of money from stocks to bonds is known as *flight to quality*, because investors seek safer, higher quality investments for their money.

One way investors keep track of what is happening in the bond market is to keep a watchful eye on the U.S. government bond called the *30-year Treasury Bond*, also known as the *long bond*. The interest rate or *yield* (as it is called) of this bond is published every day in financial news sources. When the yield goes up, investors know that inflation may be on its way. The long bond is the basis for the interest rate home buyers have to pay on long-term mortgages, so it is very important for the ordinary consumer.   Our website, www.teenvestor.com/chapter10 will provide a link to the government website that shows the level of the long bond and other bonds issued by the U.S. government.

THE MEANING OF A BOND RALLY
(For the Advanced Teenvestor)

When you hear that the "stock market rallied," it means that stock prices have moved up. This is good for people who own stocks, since they can benefit from the capital appreciation of these stocks.

But it is a bit more difficult to interpret a rally in the bond market. If you recall, a bond is basically a loan that pays interest. Corporate bonds usually pay interest twice a year to lenders.

If you own a 5-year corporate bond that pays you based on a loan of $1,000 at 10% interest, this means that you will get a total of $100 each year for 5 years. At the end of the fifth year, you will also get your original $1,000 back. Suppose that yesterday you bought this 5-year corporate bond for $1,000 (at an interest rate of 10%), and your friend buys a similar bond the next day but he gets a rate of only 9% because interest rates went down due to overnight action by the Federal Reserve Bank. Your bond is worth more because you are getting an interest rate of 10%, which is higher than the current rate of 9% any other bondholder will get if he purchased the same type of bond today.

The basic concept here is that once you own a bond that has a set interest rate, your bond looks better and better (i.e. it is worth more and more if you want to sell it) if interest rates go down. (Remember that your interest rate is already fixed, so it won't go down as long as you own it). As rates go down, your bond rallies or is worth more and more. To make a long story short, lower interest rates make bonds you own worth more. In other words, bonds rally with lower rates.

STOCK INDUSTRY GROUP

One concept you will frequently encounter as a Teenvestor is industry groupings. An industry represents a business category such as entertainment, real estate, banking, and so on. Investors typically look at companies in the same industry in the same way. For example, if the stock of J.P. Morgan Chase is doing really well, investors would expect other banks to do well also; otherwise, they'd suspect something might be wrong with a bank that does poorly compared with its peers. Industry categories are also important because they can help you decide which businesses are growing and which ones are dying.

Just because you pick a stock you are interested in buying doesn't mean that you can ignore all other stocks in the same industry. Whenever you start researching the stock of a particular company, you have to make a list of other companies in the same industry so that you can make reasonable comparisons. These comparisons are important, because most investors tend to look at companies in the same industry in the same way. For example, they will look at how much revenue and profit companies in the same industry make, how much money they owe, and other comparisons. A good example will be a comparison of the earnings of McDonald's and Wendy's, which are both in the fast food business.

One way to understand the importance of comparing companies within industries is to think of runners and the various skills needed for individual events. You wouldn't expect a 100-meter runner to do well in a 10,000-meter (6.2 miles) race, because each event requires different skills: the 100-meter runner needs a burst of speed to win his race, while the 10,000-meter runner needs a lot more endurance to finish and win his race. It would be impossible to decide who is a better athlete, the sprinter or the long-distance runner, because the events are totally different. You can, however, state that the 100-meter runner is better or worse than other 100-meter runners based on his speed. You *can* say that the 10,000-meter runner is better or worse than other long-distance runners who specialize in the same event. Just as you have to compare athletes in the same events, you have to compare companies in the same industries.

Investors think of industries as they would of a human being. A newborn baby has to be fed and clothed by his parents. This is much like a new industry that needs a lot of money at the beginning before it can even begin to make profits for its investors. In business language this is called the *early development stage*.

The baby starts to walk and feed himself and then quickly grows into a vibrant young child, and then moves through his teenage years. This is much like an industry that is developing quickly and begins selling a lot of its products and services (even though it may still not be making much profit). This is known as the *growth stage*.

The young man marries, starts a family, and watches his children graduate from high school and college. This stage is like an industry that is maturing, attracting a steady stream of customers, and making steady money for its owners. In business language, this is called the *mature* or *mature growth stage*.

The man eventually begins to feel the aches and pains of old age such as bad knees, a bad back, and other diseases associated with aging bodies. This is like an industry that has fully matured and is in decline. In business language, this is known as the *decline stage*.

If science develops cures for some of the diseases suffered by the elderly, the man could live a relatively healthy life for a long time. This is like a declining industry that has found ways to keep its products or services fresh. In business language, this is known as the *stabilization stage*. The decline stage and the stabilization stage go hand in hand, because stabilization slows the decline of an industry.

No one can really tell exactly how long each stage will last or how quickly an industry will move from one stage to another. What's important is that you know that companies have their own cycles, and you'd want to avoid putting money into declining industries.

Sometimes companies make so many types of products that it is hard to tell exactly how to categorize them in terms of industry. The general rule of thumb, however, is to put them in categories closest to what they are known for producing.

The Internet is useful for identifying industry categories of public companies. In fact, some websites such as InvestorGuide or Yahoo!Finance provide a list of companies in any given industry, and they can even give you averages of important industry information.

DIVERSIFICATION

You have probably heard of the old saying, "don't put all your eggs in one basket." When choosing stocks, investors try to invest in a few different companies so that a loss of value in one stock doesn't affect their whole *portfolio* (the basket of stocks and other investments). The act of investing in several different types of stocks to achieve this goal is called *diversification*.

Investors diversify their portfolios because when a stock goes down or rises in value, other stocks in the same industry tend to do the same. This means that if General Motors stock goes down, the stock of Fiat Chrysler is also likely to be lower, because both companies are in the automobile industry. Investors diversify by buying the stocks of companies in different industries so as to reduce the chance that the entire portfolio will lose too much value if one industry has a problem. So, for example, an investor might include the following stocks in a portfolio: General Motors (car industry), IBM (computer industry), and McDonald's (food industry). Because these stocks are all in different industries, it is unlikely that a problem in one company will affect the other two companies.

Teenvestors find it hard to diversify because they have very little money to invest. Nevertheless, it is important to know the value of not putting all your eggs in one basket if you ever get enough cash to spread your investment around to different stocks. If you are forced to invest in just one or two stocks, you then have to make sure that the stocks are as safe as possible.

BETA - HOW THE RISK OF STOCKS IS MEASURED
(For the Advanced Teenvestor)

The risk of stocks has a special name in the world of finance – *beta*. The simplified explanation of beta is that it tells you how the value of a stock moves up and down with an index like the S&P 500. You don't really have to know how it is calculated, but knowing the beta for each stock gives you an idea of how risky it is. If a stock has a beta of 1, it means that its value moves up and down by the same percentage as a market index like the S&P 500. A stock that moves with this index is said to have the same risk as the market. For example, if the S&P 500 index has a value of 5,000 today and moves to 5,500 tomorrow, this represents a 10% increase. If the stock of company XYZ has a beta of 1, you would expect its value to also increase by approximately 10%. A stock like this with a beta of 1 is not really considered risky when compared with the overall stock market. A stock with a beta of, say, 2 means that each time the S&P Index moves up by 10% or so, the stock of company XYZ moves up by 2 x 10% = 20%. It also means that this same stock can move down 20% in value if the S&P drops 10%. So in general, high beta stocks are riskier than low beta stocks. But some people like risk because, even though they can lose a lot of money, they can also gain a lot if the market goes their way.

THE BUSINESS CYCLE

Professional investors on Wall Street and other financial centers around the world view the market as having some type of pattern, which they call the *business cycle*. They observe that businesses (as reflected in the stock market) swing from good times to bad times in a fairly regular manner. There are four major parts of the business cycle: *maturation, contraction* (or *recession*), *revival*, and *expansion*. The economy flows through the four sections of this business cycle, and the way this happens is worthy of an explanation.

Let's say that we are at the stage of the business cycle where things are going great. The Dow and the S&P 500 are flying high. (In common business language, when the stock market is booming, investment experts refer to this as a *bull market*). Businesses can't keep up with the demand for their products – they can't supply enough for consumers. They have to borrow money to invest in more equipment to expand their production capabilities. They have to hire more people to make the products and pay them more, because they are competing with other companies that also want to hire more people. This stage of the business cycle is known as the maturation stage.

The maturation stage might go on for a long time, but at some point, inflation arises because more people are employed at higher costs, and the costs of materials go up (since companies are buying more and more materials to make their products). This, of course, affects how much profit companies make, since their expenses are going up faster than they can increase the price of the items they are selling. Rising inflation (and hence, rising interest rates) sets the groundwork for the next stage of the business cycle: the contraction or recession stage.

In the contraction stage, inflation, and all the bad things it brings, causes businesses to pull back. They pull back also because they have probably overbuilt factories and bought too many machines to make their products in anticipation of continued demand. With profits going down, they cut back on their equipment purchases, lay off some of the extra workers (especially those hired when things were going great and there was no inflation), cut back on salaries, and take other actions to stop their profits from declining further. With reduced incomes, consumers (or workers) reduce their spending. The stock market indexes enter a downward phase, or a *bear market* as it is commonly called. In this stage of the business cycle, businesses and consumers do not borrow as much money to buy equipment and other items. The Federal Reserve may even step in and reduce rates (by lowering the discount rate) to encourage borrowing and spending.

At some point in the recession and contraction phase, things start to turn around. The stock market, after prices have gone down due to reduced profits, begins to move up again. Recall that rates are low at this point (due to the actions of the Federal Reserve), so people are willing to give up the low rates in bonds to move back into stocks.

This sets the stage for the next phase of the business cycle – the revival stage.

In the revival stage, consumers start to feel more confident that the worst is behind them, and they start to spend again. Economic indicators like the GDP start to move higher after long periods of decline, employment numbers start to look good again, some businesses start to spend more money again. So after months or years of being in the doldrums, things begin to improve. This creates conditions for the next stage of the business cycle – the expansion stage.

In the expansion stage, the revival continues and many more businesses benefit from a good economy, not just a few businesses in specific industries. Companies that require heavy investments, such as housing construction companies and appliance manufacturers, fully benefit from a good economy. The bull market is back.

The next stage after expansion is the maturation stage. And we are right back where we started, with the economy humming, and the Dow and the S&P 500 making investors very happy.

In truth, it is sometimes difficult to tell when the economy makes the transition from the expansion to the maturation stage (although the Federal Reserve can help a bit to prolong the expansion).

A contraction stage is easier to spot. A high unemployment rate and other signs of stress in the economy can give you a clue about when contraction has set in. We witnessed such a severe contraction during "The Great Recession" that occurred in 2008, with accelerating job loss and the GDP on its way to extremely low levels.

Suppose you knew the exact time a stock would hit its lowest and highest levels in the business cycle. If you knew the exact pattern of a business cycle, you would want to buy the stock at its lowest level and sell it at its highest level (when the Dow and the S&P 500 are at their highest and are just about to come down). As a Teenvestor, you can make a fortune if you have the skill to predict the length of the cycles. Unfortunately, no one knows how long each stage of the business cycle will last. In addition, no two business cycles have exactly the same pattern. Therefore, you can't just use a calendar to tell when a new business cycle will begin and end. At the time of this writing, experts say that we are in the midst of a 10-year expansion, the longest in the history of the United States. Of course, no one knows when this stage of the cycle will end and move into the maturity and contraction stages.

It is worth repeating that the Federal Reserve tries to moderate the good times in the market by raising and lowering the discount rate. However, despite its efforts, business cycles still occur, although not necessarily with the same sting to the economy. The Federal Reserve simply tries to soften the blow when things are bad and, at the same time, makes sure that the good times don't get out of hand (which can cause more inflation). When the Fed slows an overheated economy down without causing a recession, this is known as a *soft landing*.

EXPECTATIONS VERSUS REALITY

In the previous chapter, we discussed some of the government data that affect the market. For example, we talked about how high employment can start inflation because it means that there are more people with money to spend, and this drives prices up. We want to, once again, emphasize why the market sometimes does not behave the way you might expect it to with the announcement of some economic news. The government's economic data affect stock prices only if the numbers the government is expected to publish differ from the numbers it actually publishes. This is very important to understand, so we will go through it more slowly here, even though we discussed it in the previous chapter.

At any given time, financial experts (and other professional investors) guess at the economic numbers the government will publish. Some of these experts work in companies such as Goldman Sachs and J.P. Morgan Chase that spend millions trying to predict what the GDP, inflation (the CPI), the discount rate and employment rates will be the next time the government publishes these numbers. At the same time, other people involved in the market, such as stockbrokers, form their own opinions. Eventually, all these opinions come together and reporters will say things like "analysts say that the unemployment numbers, which will be published by the U.S. Department of Labor next week, will be 4.2% for November," or "Wall Street expects the Federal Reserve to raise the discount rate by 1/4 of a percent." Remember that even though these are only the opinions of the experts, these opinions can affect the market immediately, even before the actual figures are published. When the government publishes the true numbers, a couple of things can happen. If the government's numbers match what the experts predict, the stock market will probably not move very much. If, however, the actual numbers are worse than or better than predicted, the stock market will move in one direction or another. Therefore, the difference between expected economic figures and what the economic figures actually turn out to be is the key to the changing fortunes of the stock market. For example, if the market has already assumed that the Fed is going to raise rates, stock prices will have already adjusted (in anticipation of a rate hike) before the Federal Reserve acts.

THE VARIOUS STOCK CLASSIFICATIONS

Investors love to put stocks into various categories to make it easier to identify them. There are probably more than a dozen stock classifications, but we will describe only the following five here: *blue-chip*, *growth*, *income*, *cyclical*, and *interest-rate-sensitive* stocks.

Blue-chip stocks are stocks of the biggest companies in the country. They are usually the stocks of high-quality companies with years of strong profit and steady dividend payments. They are also some of the safest stocks in which to invest. You will probably not get rich overnight by investing in these stocks, but you will sleep better knowing that you won't lose your hard-earned money, either. The stocks that are part of the Dow, for example, are considered blue-chip stocks.

Growth stocks are stocks of companies with profits that are increasing quickly. This increase in profits is reflected in the rise in the company's stock price. The definition of the level of profit increase that marks a growth stock varies from time to time. At this writing, however, net profit growth of 15% to 20% is the standard. Just as a tree can't grow to the heavens, a stock can't grow forever. At some point, the growth rate will slow to a modest rate of 10% or less.

A growth company usually spends a lot of money on research and puts all its profits back into the company instead of paying dividends. In addition, it usually sells unique products, and these days, it is likely to be a high-technology company that depends on intellectual power (such as software companies). Some software, Internet, and other computer-related companies can be considered growth companies. While the stock prices of growth companies increase more rapidly than the stocks of some blue-chip companies, they are also riskier because their prices can tumble just as quickly as they rise.

Income stocks are the stocks of stable companies that pay large dividends. Older people who are retired often buy stocks in these stable companies, since it provides them with a steady income that's also more than they can earn by investing in bonds or putting their money in savings accounts. These investors are more interested in getting cash in their hands to meet their modest lifestyles than in holding the more risky growth stocks. Institutions such as colleges also put their money in income stocks to provide them with a steady stream of dividends to keep their doors open, instead of depending on stock prices to go up. The stocks of electric utility companies are typically considered income stocks.

Cyclical stocks are stocks in companies whose fortunes go up and down with the business cycle. Stock prices of these companies go up when general business conditions are good (as reflected by a bull market), and the prices go down when general business conditions are bad (such as in a bear market). Cyclical companies usually invest in heavy equipment to make their products, and they are known for laying people off when business is down. Cyclical companies can be found in the following types of industries: paper, chemicals, steel, machinery and machine tools, airlines, railroads and railroad equipment, and automobiles.

Interest-rate sensitive stocks are affected primarily by changes in interest rates. Banks and other financial companies can be considered interest-rate sensitive companies. These companies feel the effects of any move by the Federal Reserve to hold off inflation or to kick-start the economy.

STOCK INVESTMENT APPROACHES

Investors have two major classifications for their investment methods: *growth* investing and *value* investing. Most people use investment strategies that combine both growth and value investing.

Not surprisingly, growth investors look for growth companies as described in the previous section. Often they look for stock prices that are shooting up; that is, they look for *momentum* (otherwise known as forward movement) in these stocks. The stock prices may be high compared with the earnings of the companies, but growth investors don't care. Growth investors also tend to trade a lot of shares in and out of their portfolios. They keep an eye on their stock prices and sell their shares as soon as they see slowing growth in the companies in which they have invested.

Value investors sometimes look for stocks that have fallen on hard times, and therefore are relatively cheap compared with their prior prices. They also look for stocks that have been overlooked by other investors for one reason or another. In other words, they are looking for a bargain and hoping to buy shares before prices go up (when more people realize that the stock is a bargain).

RETURN ON INVESTMENT

One of the most basic financial concepts is *return on investment* or ROI. Return on investment measures how much profit you have gained or lost (in percentage terms) by investing in stocks, mutual funds, bonds, a business venture, a bank account, or any other type of financial product. When you put your money in a bank account that pays interest, you are making a loan to the bank for which you get a small profit as interest. Your investment is the loan to the bank, and the return on your investment is the interest rate paid by the bank.

The return on investment for a stock is not guaranteed in the way that a bank deposit is. For stocks, the return on investment depends on how much stock prices increase after you've bought your shares. In general, the return of a stock and other investments that are held for one year can be calculated as follows:

ROI = [(End Value - Beginning Value) / (Beginning Value)] x 100

Where End Value is the price received for selling the investment.

Where Beginning Value is the price you paid when you purchased the investment. (We assume there are no fees charged by anyone who helped you buy or sell the investment).

So if you bought a share of stock for $50 and sold it one year later for $60, your return can be calculated as follows:

ROI = [($60-$50) / ($50)] x 100 = [($10) / ($50)] x 100 = 20% per year

Return on investment gets slightly more complicated if you hold the investment for less than one year or for longer than one year. We will spare you the agony of the mathematics here; you can learn more about it on www.teenvestor.com.

COMPOUNDING (For the Advanced Teenvestor)

Compounding refers to the rate at which money grows if you automatically reinvest all the profit you make in the same investment. To help you understand the concept of compounding, we will use a simple example of a bank account that pays interest. A bank can pay you two kinds of interest: simple interest or compound interest. Suppose you have $1,000 in the bank that pays 10% simple interest per year for 10 years. Each year, you will earn $100 interest on your $1,000 investment (in the bank account) as calculated below:

Yearly Interest = Yearly Interest Percentage x Deposit Amount

Yearly Interest = 10% x $1,000 = 0.1 x $1,000 = $100

The yearly simple interest for the 10-year period is shown below:

	Simple Interest		Principal Balance		Interest Earned on Principal
1.	10%	x	$1,000.00	=	$100
2.	10%	x	$1,000.00	=	$100
3.	10%	x	$1,000.00	=	$100
4.	10%	x	$1,000.00	=	$100
5.	10%	x	$1,000.00	=	$100
6.	10%	x	$1,000.00	=	$100
7.	10%	x	$1,000.00	=	$100
8.	10%	x	$1,000.00	=	$100
9.	10%	x	$1,000.00	=	$100
10.	10%	x	$1,000.00	=	$100
					$1,000

As you can see, the total amount of simple interest earned in the 10-year period is $1,000. We calculated this amount by multiplying the yearly interest of 10% by the initial amount you deposited in your account (the *principal balance* of $1,000) and adding up the resulting products for the 10-year period. Since you get back your initial principal balance of $1,000, you will receive a total of $2,000 at the end of the 10-year period. Remember that this simple interest method shown in the example above assumes that your yearly profit of $100 is not reinvested into the account.

If the bank tells you that you will earn 10% yearly compound interest on your deposit (instead of 10% simple interest), you will make more on your investment than in the simple interest case. Once again, on a yearly basis, you will be earning 10% profit on your principal. But the difference in this case is that your yearly profit (i.e. your yearly interest) will be reinvested each year into the bank account, and not taken out, as was the case with the simple interest calculation above. Here is how your money will stack up each year with compound interest:

	Compound Interest		Principal Balance		Interest Earned on Principal
1.	10%	X	$1,000.00	=	$100.00
2.	10%	X	$1,100.00	=	$110.00
3.	10%	X	$1,210.00	=	$121.00
4.	10%	X	$1,331.00	=	$133.10
5.	10%	X	$1,464.00	=	$146.40
6.	10%	X	$1,610.50	=	$161.05
7.	10%	X	$1,771.60	=	$177.16
8.	10%	X	$1,948.70	=	$194.87
9.	10%	X	$2,143.60	=	$214.36
10.	10%	X	$2,357.90	=	$235.79
					$1,593.73

With yearly compounding, the interest earned in one year is reinvested into the bank account in the next year. You can tell that this is the case because the Principal Balance column above is increasing, so interest is applied to a bigger and bigger principal balance each year. With the yearly compound interest method, the principal balance increases from $1,000 in the first year to $2,357.90 in the tenth year. With the simple interest method, the principal balance stays at $1,000 for all ten years. At the end of the tenth year for the yearly compound interest example, the total interest earned is $1,593.73 as opposed to $1,000 with simple interest—a difference of $593.73.

Compounding can be done yearly (as is the case in our example), monthly, daily, or in any other time interval. Once again, we will spare you the agony of the mathematics here, but we can show you how it is done on www.teenvestor.com/chapter10 if you are curious.

In our prior two examples, the total compound interest was higher than the total simple interest by $593.73. This may seem like a small number, but remember that we assumed you deposited only $1,000 for a 10-year period. As the initial deposit balance increases, the difference between compounding interest and simple interest gets bigger and bigger. And the longer the money stays in the account (or in the investment), the bigger the difference.

The reason we are telling you all of this is because compounding also has a big effect on the money you put into stocks, bonds, mutual funds, and other investments. We will now apply this concept to the return on investment in stocks.

Recall from our introduction that over the past 90 years, the average return on investment for stocks was around 11% per year. This means that on the average, someone investing in stocks (and reinvesting all her dividends as well) could have made 11% profit each year over a long, long time. Because of the compounding effect of investments, a long-term investor can double her money every seven or eight years if we assume an 11% annual profit. Imagine the profit if the investment balance were bigger. This multiplication effect of invested money is one of the reasons it is wise to invest for the long run. We will explain more about this concept in a later chapter.

The power of compounding is so important to investors that a formula called *the rule of 72* has been devised to tell any investor about how much time it will take to double her money, given a yearly compound rate. The rule of 72 states that if you divide 72 by an assumed compound rate, you would get the approximate number of years it will take to double your money. The formula is as follows:

Time to Double Your Money = 72 / Interest Rate

So, if the compound rate is 11%, the formula is as follows:

Time to Double Your Money = 72 / 11 = 6.55 years

Thus, the approximate time to double your money at a compound rate of 11% per year is 6.55 years (or about 7 years). At a compound rate of 22% per year, it will take about 3.27 years (72 / 22 = 3.27 years).

THE TIME VALUE OF MONEY
(For the Advanced Teenvestor)

The *time value of money* is another very important investing concept. The application of this idea is what determines your parents' monthly mortgage, car loan payment, or installment loan payments. It also has an effect on the price of stocks.

Time value of money simply says that a dollar received today is worth more than a dollar received in one day, one month, or a year, because the dollar received today can start earning interest immediately. It is such a simple idea that you probably already know it, but you just haven't thought about how it can affect your actions. Let's consider an example of how this idea can be applied.

Suppose someone told you that you could have $100,000 today or $105,000 a year from now (assuming you have no immediate need for the money). Which would you prefer?

You cannot really answer this question until we supply you with one more piece of information: the return you could earn in one year by putting the $100,000 in an alternate investment. You could easily answer the question if you knew that you could put the $100,000 you'd receive today in a bank account paying 10% yearly compound interest.

Think about the choices again: receive $100,000 today or receive $105,000 one year from now. For those of you who would rather have the $105,000 one year from now, you would have cheated yourself out of $5,000. If you collect $100,000 today, you can deposit it in the bank and earn 10% interest for the year, or $10,000, on that money. In one year, you would have a principal and interest total of $110,000. This is $5,000 more than you would get if you'd opted to receive $105,000 one year in the future.

If we told you that you could have $100,000 today or $110,000 one year from now, both choices are equivalent, because the extra $10,000 we would give you one year from now exactly equals the amount of money you could earn by investing $100,000 in the bank for one year.

This time value of money idea means that if you have a choice of receiving money today or a year from now, the money you expect a year from now should be higher than the money you are offered today.

Turning the situation around a bit, suppose someone told you that you are eligible to receive $100,000 one year from now. At the same time, she asked you how much money you'd require today such that you'd give up the $100,000 you could receive in a year. Once again, this would depend on how much you could earn by investing the money you would get today for one year. Let's go through the numbers.

Assume again that the interest rate you would get by putting your money in a bank is a 10% yearly compound rate. The question you have to ask yourself is: how much would I have to put in a bank account that pays 10% yearly compound interest such that at the end of one year, I'd have $100,000? Mathematically, the equation to solve is as follows:

Future Value = (Present Value) + (Present Value) x (Rate on Investment)

Where Future Value is the amount of money you would get in the future, which is $100,000 in our example.

Where Present Value is the amount of money you would need today such that if you invested it in a bank today, you would end up with the Future Value.

Where Rate on Investment is the interest rate you would be paid for your investment, which is 10% in our example.

What we are trying to figure out in the equation above is Present Value – how much you would need today such that if you invest it, you would end up with $100,000 in a year. We can easily solve the equation as follows:

Future Value = (Present Value) + (Present Value) x (Rate on Investment)

With a bit of manipulation, we get the following formula:

Future Value = (Present Value) x (1 + Rate on Investment)

With more manipulation, we get the following formula:

Present Value = Future Value / (1 + Rate on Investment)

Substituting the numbers in our example, we get the following equation:

Present Value = $100,000 / (1 + 10%) = $100,000 / (1 + .1) = $100,000 / 1.1
Present Value = $90,909.09

Remember the original question: how much cash would you require today such that you would not have to be paid $100,000 one year from now? As you can see from the formula above, the answer is that you should require at least $90,909.09 today, and we can prove it. With $90,909.09 on hand today, you could put it in a bank account earning 10% per year. The total amount of money you would have in one year if you invest this money in the bank (Future Value) would be calculated as follows:

Future Value = $90,909.09 + ($90,909.09) x (10%)
Future Value = $90,909.09 + $9090.909 = $100,000

If we changed the original question and asked how much cash you would require today such that you would not have to be paid $100,000 two years from now, the answer gets slightly more complicated, but the basic principle is the same. You just need to know how much money you would need today such that if you earn 10% interest in the first year, and another 10% interest in the second year, you would end up with $100,000. Without going through the mathematics, the answer is $82,644.63. We can prove it as follows:

Year#1 Future Value = $82,644.63 + ($82,644.63) x (10%) = $90,909.09

The investment balance for the second year's investment is now $90,909.09, so at the end of the second year, you would end up with:

Year#2 Future Value = $90,909.09 + ($90,909.09) x (10%) = $100,000

So as you can see, you should require $82,644.63 today such that you would give up $100,000 two years from now. Notice that we have quietly used the compounding concept here, because we assumed that in the second year, the new invested balance includes the interest earned in the first year.

The terms *present value* and *future value* have very special meanings in the investment world. Present value refers to today's value of a sum of money to be received in the future. If someone asks you for the present value of $100,000, you would need two pieces of additional information from them: how far in the future the money will be received and the rate of investment [or *discount rate*, as it is commonly known in finance lingo when calculating present value (not to be confused with the Federal Reserve Bank's discount rate discussed in Chapter 9)] that is to be applied. In our example, the present value of $100,000 to be received in two years, and to which a discount rate of 10% is applied, was $82,644.63. Though we didn't show you the calculation for this, the present value of $100,000 to be received in 50 years and to which a 10% discount rate is to be applied is $852.86. That's correct – if someone gave you $852.86 today, you would get $100,000 back in 50 years if the compound interest rate or discount rate were assumed to be 10%.

Future value is easier to understand because you are already used to calculating it whether you know it or not. Future value is how much you would earn by making an investment today and collecting your money in the future. Like present value, you will need to know the rate of investment and the amount of time in which you will receive the cash. When calculating future value, however, the rate of investment is known as the *investment rate* – the percentage return (like the interest in our bank deposit example). So, the future value of $82,644.63 in two years, assuming a 10% compound investment rate, is $100,000 (as we calculated earlier). Though we didn't show you the calculation for this, the future value of $100,000 to be received in 50 years, assuming a 10% compound investment rate, is $11,739,085.

HOW THE TIME VALUE OF MONEY AND STOCK PRICES ARE RELATED (For the Advanced Teenvestor)

In Chapter 9, we briefly mentioned how inflation affects the stock market, but we didn't really give you a full explanation. We can now give you the details here because we've covered the meaning of present value.

In general, stock prices depend on how much investors expect companies to make in the future. You can think of the change in the price of a stock as the result of a vote by investors on whether they think the company will make more or less money in the future. If more investors think the company will do better in the future than those who think the company will do worse in the future, the price of a stock will go up because of the law of supply and demand as discussed earlier in the chapter. Likewise, if more investors think the company will do worse in the future than those who think the company will do better, the price of a stock will go down.

When you add the element of inflation, the movement in the price of a stock gets more interesting. The higher the inflation rate, the smaller the present value of a company's future earnings, because inflation increases the discount rate to be applied to the company's future earnings. If you recall our previous discussion, the present value of money to be received in the future is as follows:

Present Value = Future Value / (1 + Rate on Investment)
Where Rate on Investment is the discount rate

As the denominator of the equation above increases (that is, as the discount rate increases), the present value of the company's future earnings gets smaller and smaller. What this means is that a company's future earnings are worth less and less as inflation creeps up, because inflation is reflected in the discount rate – the higher the inflation, the higher the discount rate. This is the main reason why investors hate inflation.

For more information, website links, videos, and any assignments associated with this chapter, please visit:

www.teenvestor.com/chapter10

11

HOW TO FIND THE RIGHT STOCK

There are probably more than 10,000 stocks you can buy for your investment portfolio. There is no way you can investigate each of these stocks to see which ones are likely to increase in value. Our general view is that Teenvestors should invest in what they know *and* in products in which they have an interest, at least at the beginning of their life-long investment efforts. The important thing is to get started buying the stocks of big companies that will be around for a long time.

It is also important to make a habit of investing in stocks at regular intervals. Once a month, two times a year – it doesn't matter as long as you make it a priority to put your money in stocks that are likely to grow.

As a beginning investor, you should try as much as possible to stick to the companies in the Dow or the largest companies in the S&P 500. However, if you have trouble getting motivated, we have a few suggestions to help you decide which stocks to consider buying after doing the fundamental research described in Chapters 12 and 13.

THE BUSINESSES IN WHICH YOUR RELATIVES WORK

Unless your parents work for the government, you can get good investment ideas by talking to them about the companies and the industries in which they work to see whether these companies are good investment opportunities. They can tell you whether their companies are doing innovative things that will make for attractive investments. Ask your parents to show you any annual reports or brochures the company produces for the public. Your parents can give you some insight on the trends in the industry, the competitors, and the general feelings of the employees in the company. Keep in mind, however, that there is a limit to the information your parents are allowed to pass on to you. This is because employees who come in possession of material non-public information (called *insider information*) cannot benefit financially from that information.

Don't just stop with your parents. Your other relatives, your neighbors, and your friends' parents have a wealth of knowledge you can tap to learn about what is going on in different industries. They can alert you to trends before everyone else knows about them. Make a habit of asking about the businesses they are in and about any exciting products or services their companies are developing. Once again, you can ask these relatives and acquaintances about annual reports and other publicly available information that may help you understand the industries in which they work.

Speaking of friends and relatives, you should do your own research before making any purchases. Some people have a habit of boasting about their great investments without mentioning their losses in the market. There are no sure things when it comes to investing in the stock market.

CONSIDER YOUR HOBBIES

Hobbies are often a good place to start looking for investment opportunities. If your hobby is collectibles, for example, you may be interested in learning more about companies that specialize in sports memorabilia, art, toys, and other collectibles for hobbyists. You can probably find a stock associated with any kind of hobby you can imagine. If you like longboarding, you can find a company that makes the equipment, the pads, and other items associated with the activity. If you like sports, there are lots of publicly traded companies that make sporting equipment.

To recap, our philosophy is that following your interests is a possible way for you can get motivated to begin investing. You may not make any profit and you may even lose money, but this will at least get you acclimated to the market. When you become an experienced Teenvestor, you can then move on to investments in big companies that look promising – whether you have a passion for those businesses or not.

LOOK TO YOUR FRIENDS AND CLASSMATES FOR IDEAS

Other young people are excellent sources of good investment ideas. Just by observing what your friends and classmates love to wear and eat, you can see some good investment potential. The entertainment they choose and the beverages they drink can also be a clue to the right stocks. For example, if you notice that your classmates prefer energy drinks, perhaps this is a sign that you should look more carefully into the stock performance of companies that make such beverages. Look around your school for items that are popular among your classmates. Look around your house for products, foods, and gadgets that your family prefers. Ideas are everywhere. Don't limit yourself to just what is in your immediate environment. The only things to watch out for are items that are too trendy, because they will probably fade away in a year or two.

START READING BUSINESS PUBLICATIONS

Teenvestors should read business publications available in print or online. Fortunately, 13-year olds can read and understand most general business publications. We knew an 11-year old who read *The Wall Street Journal* regularly.

We believe *The Wall Street Journal* should be required reading for every Teenvestor. Go to the publication's website and just review the short article summaries if you don't have a paid subscription – you are sure to absorb something from this great publication. In addition, high-quality business news aggregators and publications such as Yahoo!Finance, Marketwatch, Investopedia, *Forbes*, and *Fortune* can be great resources on new companies and trends you should explore for investment ideas. These publications can often save Teenvestors lots of research time because they publish detailed, up-to-date articles on some of the biggest companies in the United States and around the world.

There are also some relatively new publications such as *TechCrunch, GeekWire,* and *VentureBeat* that specialize in articles about technology companies. Although we feel that high-technology investing is for the advanced Teenvestor, you may want to sample some of these magazines as well.

Here is a list of some news and information sources that will help anyone age 12 or older to become a true Teenvestor:

The Wall Street Journal (wsj.com)
Yahoo!Finance (finance.yahoo.com)
MarketWatch (marketwatch.com)
CBS Moneywatch (cbsmoneywatch.com)
Financial Times (ft.com)
Bloomberg (bloomberg.com)
Fortune (fortune.com)
Forbes (forbes.com)
CNN Money (money.cnn.com)
Fast Company (fastcompany.com)
TechCrunch (techcrunch.com)
GeekWire (geekwire.com)
VentureBeat (venturebeat.com)
The Economist (economist.com)
Seeking Alpha (seekingalpha.com)

In addition to these publications and websites, most major online news publications have excellent business sections. Some of these are: the *New York Times,* the *Washington Post, USA Today,* the *San Francisco Chronicle,* and many others.

LOOK AT THE COMPANIES HEADQUARTERED IN YOUR STATE

If you look around, you will notice there are some big companies with headquarters in your state. This is probably no surprise if you live in the northeastern states such as New York, New Jersey, Pennsylvania, or Massachusetts, or in other large states such as California or Texas. But states with smaller populations also have sizable corporations. Because these companies are in your state (or in some cases, in your city), your family may even know people who work for them and can help you decide whether they are good candidates for your investment dollar. The annual *Fortune 500* edition of *Fortune* magazine usually lists the biggest companies in the U.S. by geographical areas. You should be able to find the list online.

TRY CHOOSING SPECIFIC INDUSTRIES

Another way to determine which companies are worth investing in is to identify *industry* and *sector* categories that interest you. An industry category defines the line of business a company is in. For example, Apple is in the electronic equipment industry. A sector identifies major categories that industries can be slotted into. In other words, industries are subsets of sectors. While Apple is in the electronic equipment industry, its sector is consumer goods. Classifying stock is useful if, through your research and reading of business publications, you determine that a particular industry or sector will be a good investment, but you don't know exactly which companies in that industry or sector will make for the best investments. Knowing the industry or sector of the company in which you want to invest also makes it easier for you to compare how the company is doing relative to its competitors. We use the stock sectors and industries as classified by Yahoo!Finance in our analyses of stocks. Yahoo!Finance has nine sectors and more than 200 industry categories. Many other organizations, such as Standard & Poor's, Moody's, and Morningstar have their own industry categories, although the major sectors from one organization to another are quite similar.

AVOID INVESTMENT IDEAS FROM SOCIAL MEDIA

There are lots of online forums that discuss investments. In addition, stock tips and commentary circulate on social media. Some people probably get good investment ideas from these sources, but some of the participants are known to work for (or manage) companies on which they are commenting. In addition, any fool with fingers can type advice online for hundreds of thousands of people to read. We recommend that you stay away from online investment ideas offered by people you don't know.

In 2000, 15-year-old Jonathan Lebed became the youngest person ever charged with violating Securities and Exchange Commission (SEC) regulations. The SEC, the law enforcement organization for the financial markets, accused Jonathan of involvement in a "pump and dump" scheme. The organization claimed that Jonathan posted messages in chat rooms touting stocks of very tiny companies that he happened to have invested in. As people who believed him bought the stocks, he quietly sold (i.e., dumped) the shares he owned because they were worth more after he pumped up their value on the

Internet. According to the SEC, Jonathan made more than $800,000 with this scheme. He settled the case with the SEC without admitting or denying guilt, but the case illustrates how people can be fooled into buying stock by listening to online "experts."

If you need more reasons not to chat or tweet your way into investing, how about two words: *insider trading*. Insider trading is when you use important information that is not public (that is, the company has not released the information to the general public) to make money. In 2000, the U.S. government for the first time charged a group of people, who met in social media, with sharing insider information on the Internet. One man passed information to another, and another, and it mushroomed from there. Everyone who got information and bought stock based on that information, whether the information was from the initial source or not, was held responsible by the government. The SEC's job has gotten much tougher since this early pursuit of insider traders; they now include hackers who break into corporate computers to get confidential information on which they can trade. In a recent *Forbes* article titled *Hackers Bring Insider Trading to the Internet Age*, the publication stated the following about Federal officials chasing such hackers:

> According to the two indictments released by prosecutors, the defendants allegedly orchestrated a scheme in which computer hackers based abroad obtained 150,000 corporate press releases prior to their public distribution. With early access to major news events like quarterly earnings reports or merger announcements, it was easy for the traders in the operation to earn illegal profits by trading on stocks before anyone else received the news.

Such hacking activities also increase the chances that you may inadvertently come upon information online that is considered insider information, and this may put you in jeopardy of being charged with insider trading if you act on such illegally obtained information.

For more information, website links, videos, and any assignments associated with this chapter, please visit:

www.teenvestor.com/chapter11

TeenVestor

12

EVALUATING STOCKS: UNDERSTANDING WHAT COMPANIES DO

There are two approaches investors use in evaluating stocks: *fundamental analysis* and *technical analysis*. Fundamental stock analysts focus on a company's ability to grow and make more money in the future. They do so by looking at: how much money the company has made in the past, how much money it has borrowed, how much dividend it has paid to investors, how good its managers are, and other things that may affect the company's long-term profitability. In considering how good a company's managers are, a fundamental analyst might look at the qualifications of a new chief executive officer (CEO). If the new CEO is coming from another company that he whipped into shape and made more profitable, this is great news for the fundamental analyst, who would be optimistic that this CEO will do wonders for his new company.

Unlike fundamental analysts, technical analysts focus on how stock prices move up and down and how many shares of a company's stock are bought and sold on a day-to-day basis. Pure technical analysts don't usually concern themselves with the company's historical earnings or how wonderful the management may be. They are more likely to chart the up and down movements of a company's stock price for a period of time. By looking at the pattern of such movements, good technical analysts can sometimes predict which direction stock prices will move. The truth is there are probably no pure fundamental or technical analysts. Fundamental analysts often apply some technical analysis, and vice versa. In this chapter, we will teach you the first rule of basic fundamental analysis: understanding what a company does.

GETTING AN OVERVIEW OF THE COMPANY

Knowing what a company does and the various businesses it is in is perhaps the most important item to understand when you begin evaluating a company. In addition, you should identify other companies that may be in the same business as the company you are investigating; this way, you can compare the company against its competitors.

The Company's Stock Symbol

Each company has a stock symbol used for identification. This symbol makes it easier to list the stock on exchanges such as the New York Stock Exchange and the NASDAQ, where stocks are bought and sold. Before you can find the stock symbol for a company, you need to know the company's proper name. Because some companies have their names boldly written on the items they sell, you can easily identify their products. For example, you can guess that Nike shoes are made by Nike. However, the names of some products are not necessarily the names of the companies that make them. For example, the snack food Doritos is made by Frito-Lay, which is owned by PepsiCo, Inc. – the same company that makes Pepsi-Cola, Mountain Dew, Sierra Mist, and Tropicana. If the product is easily available, such as candy or potato chips, you can usually find the name of the company in the small print on the container or wrapper.

If you have no clue about who makes a particular product (or delivers a particular service), you can always search for it on the Internet or look it up on Wikipedia. The result of your search should produce the names of the companies that make the products in which you might invest, and it is easy then to find the company's stock symbol on its own or any financial website.

When you type a stock symbol in the various financial websites, you will see the latest financial information about the company. The first information you are likely to see after typing in a stock symbol is the latest stock price, along with the change in price from the previous day.

The Annual Report

Once you know the company you want to invest in, you should obtain an *annual report*. This should be available online, but if not, you can call or email the *investor relations* department of the company for a copy. Annual reports are usually magazine-size booklets that public companies send out yearly to their stockholders, the media, and potential investors to tell the world how the companies are doing. They are produced a few months after the end of a company's fiscal year. Annual reports are usually written to make the companies look really good, but the Securities and Exchange Commission (SEC) requires that they provide some standard financial information.

Although you can get most of the information about any company through the Internet, we think you should keep the annual report of the company you are evaluating as a reference for your research.

Basic Description of the Company's Operation

Big companies like Ford, Coca-Cola, and J.P. Morgan Chase have traditionally provided investors with lots of information about their operations. As for the smaller and less widely known businesses, it used to be much harder to get an idea of the products or services they provide without spending lots of time in the library. Fortunately, the Internet has made gathering information about companies a lot easier.

You would think that what a company does is pretty obvious. But in some cases, it is hard to know exactly what a company does until you do more research. Take a company like General Electric (GE). Most people will tell you that GE makes appliances such as refrigerators, microwave ovens, and so on. But did you know that the company also makes aircraft engines? Don't assume you know what a company does until you do your research.

Sometimes a company can be in so many different businesses that it is hard to pinpoint what it does. We tell Teenvestors to avoid companies that go into various businesses that are not related in some way For example, if Coca-Cola decided to go into the furniture business, this would be a sure sign that the company has lost its focus.

Websites where you can do your company research have write-ups called *snapshots*, or *capsules* (or other names that give you the idea that the descriptions are summaries about the activities of public companies). You can find these summaries on most good financial websites. We often use Yahoo!Finance for such summaries.

Keep in mind that a snapshot is just the starting point for finding out what a company does. There are lots of articles in the business publications and websites we mentioned in Chapter 11 that can provide the information necessary to make intelligent decisions about investing. Many of these publications are online, and you can access them through our website.

Detailed Description of a Company's Operations
(For the Advanced Teenvestor)

Advanced Teenvestors who really want to understand the operations of a specific company can try the U.S. Securities and Exchange Commission (SEC). The SEC requires all U.S. companies that are traded on stock exchanges to file yearly and quarterly reports (called 10-Ks and 10-Qs, respectively) about their operations. These reports have a Business Section that can give you some insight about the business, the competition, the company's plans, and other interesting pieces of information that can help you determine what a company does. You can get these filings from the SEC's website (www.sec.gov). Other websites take company information from the SEC and format it to make it easier to use and understand.

Identifying the Competitors

In Chapter 10, we discussed the importance of identifying the industry category of a company in which you are considering investing. If you recall, we stated that comparing companies in the same industry is good because it can give you a yardstick with which to measure the company you are considering. For example, if you were looking at investing in McDonald's, it makes sense to also look at how Wendy's is performing. If you have no real loyalty to McDonald's and you find that Wendy's is a better company, you may want to invest in Wendy's instead.

> For more information, website links, videos, and any assignments associated with this chapter, please visit:
>
> www.teenvestor.com/chapter12

13

EVALUATING STOCKS: LOOKING AT THE NUMBERS

This chapter is primarily to help you evaluate stable companies that have been making money for a period of five years or more. The ideas presented here can't be totally applied to some newly-formed high-tech companies, although the information-gathering techniques we teach you can be used for any type of company.

As you go through the calculations in this chapter, keep in mind that most of the numbers you need to analyze a company are readily available through various investment websites. We believe, however, that you will be a better Teenvestor if you truly understand the meaning of the numbers and do some of the calculations yourself.

There is no one magical formula that will tell you whether to buy a stock or not. And despite how confident they may appear, those well-dressed experts on financial news shows can't tell you for sure whether a stock will be a loser or a winner. The best anyone can do is to point you to signs that could *possibly* mean good or bad things for a company. Remember all of this as you go through this chapter or any other investment books.

The examples we provide in this chapter primarily involve the following six companies: PepsiCo Inc., Apple Inc., McDonald's Corp., Merck & Co. Inc., Chipotle Mexican Grille Inc., and Alphabet Inc. (formerly Google Inc.). Please understand that by using these companies in our examples, we are not endorsing them as good investments. We just happened to choose them out of the thousands of large, well-known companies available to illustrate the principles discussed in this chapter.

Unless otherwise stated, we used numbers from these companies' most recent fiscal year balance sheets and income statements. (See Chapter 6 for more on fiscal years). We will update these numbers on our website, www.teenvestor.com/chapter13, as we get more up-to-date financial information.

FACTS AND FIGURES ABOUT THE COMPANY

Once you have a thorough understanding of what a company does, your next step is to look at the company's financial figures. These numbers include the size of the company, its sales or revenue, its earnings, its balance sheet components, and other significant factors that can help you decide whether to buy the company's stock.

Market Capitalization

Market capitalization (or *market cap*) gives you an indication of the size of a company. It is the number of shares held by the public times the current stock price. Mathematically, it is represented as follows:

Market Capitalization = (# of Shares) x (Current Stock Price)

As you can see from the above formula, the market cap of a company changes with its stock price. At the time of this writing, our six sample companies had the following market capitalizations:

Market Capitalization (In Billions)

PepsiCo (PEP)	Apple (AAPL)	McDonald's (MCD)	Merck (MRK)	Chipotle (CMG)	Alphabet (GOOG)
$147.30	$585.95	$110.15	$157.15	$13.09	$494.74

Investors typically use the terms *mega-cap*, *large-cap*, *mid-cap*, *small-cap*, *micro-cap*, and *nano-cap* to classify the sizes of companies. There are no clear-cut numbers for determining whether to classify a company in one category or another. The Motley Fool, a company that runs a popular investment website, suggests the following classification for the market cap of companies:

Nano-cap   less than $50 million
Micro-cap   between $50 million and $250 million
Small-cap   between $250 million and $2 billion
Mid-cap   between $2 billion and $10 billion
Large-cap   between $10 billion and $100 billion
Mega-cap   > $100 billion

We recommend that beginning Teenvestors start with large-cap or mega-cap companies because their stock prices don't go up or down as much as those of smaller companies. The general rule is that the bigger a company is, the less the stock price will move up or down. The Dow consists only of large-cap or mega-cap stocks, which generally have stable prices over a short period of time. But of course, stable prices also mean that the stocks in the Dow don't grow quickly in value either. Occasionally, large-cap stocks can go bust, as was the case in 2009 when General Motors – a company that was more than 100 years old at the time – filed for bankruptcy protection and was subsequently bailed out by the U.S. government. Over a long time, however, large-cap or mega-cap shares generally do well, except perhaps under the worst economic circumstances.

After getting your feet wet with large-cap or mega-cap companies, you can also try companies in the higher range of the mid-cap classification (i.e., market cap of between $2 billion and $10 billion). We recommend that you stay away from small-caps until you're really good at doing company research (which might be three or four years from now).

Under no circumstances should you invest in micro-cap or nano-cap stocks (which cover stocks known as *penny stocks*). Some beginning investors find penny stocks attractive because they can be bought for a few dollars per share, or even for pennies per share. But these stocks are extremely risky; it is difficult to get reliable information about such companies that can tell the investor whether their stocks are good investments or not. In fact, these types of stocks are open to fraud by brokers for reasons that are beyond the topic of this book. To put it plainly, there is a good chance you will lose your money with penny stocks unless you really know what you are doing and you have a reliable source of legitimate company information.

Sales or Revenue

Sales (also known as *revenue*) tell you the dollar amount of goods and services a company sells. This is important because it really tells you the amount of money being brought into a company as a result of its customers' desire for whatever the company is selling.

Growth of Sales

When considering whether to invest in a company, growth in sales is what really matters – not just the level of sales. Growth in sales matters because as an investor, you want to know that the demand for a company's products or services will increase. If the demand is high, the company is more likely to continue making more money. And the money a company makes helps determine its stock price.

It's important for a Teenvestor to find out why big changes in sales may happen from year to year. If the change in sales is because the company sold some of its operations to another company, then a decrease in sales doesn't mean that the company is doing poorly. If the decrease in sales is because no one wants what the company is selling, then that is bad news. Because good Teenvestors invest in stocks for the long term, small decreases in sales over a one-year or two-year period may be no big deal. It is important to know the underlying cause of the change, but there may be no need to panic with a small decrease in sales. However, if sales have been going down steadily over the past three years, we recommend that you try some other company unless you have a good reason to expect a rebound.

On the other hand, sales figures could suddenly increase for a company, not because it sold more of its goods and services, but because the company purchased or merged with another company. An increase in sales due to mergers or acquisitions doesn't tell investors anything – good or bad – about the demand for a company's products or services.

As is the case in all of our analysis, you must compare the sales growth in the company you are researching with the growth in the industry. There are websites that can give you the sales growth averages in specific industries. In general, sales growth of about 10% is considered good for large-cap companies. For mid-cap and small-cap companies, sales growth of 15% to 20% or more is ideal.

Cost of Goods Sold

While sales or revenue growth is important, the cost of making those sales, referred to as *cost of sales* or *cost of goods sold (COGS)*, is also very important. Keep in mind that cost of sales refers only to the cost of the materials or labor used to make the products sold or the services delivered. COGS does not include:

1. *Selling, General & Administrative Expenses* or SGA – expenses not directly related to the products or services sold such as rent, lease, utilities, salary (unrelated to labor costs of making the goods), marketing, etc.

2. *Research & Development* or R&D – investments companies make in developing new and better products or services.

3. *Interest, Taxes, Depreciation and Amortization* or ITDA – interest on loans, taxes owed, and depreciation and amortization on buildings and equipment.

Professional investors pay close attention to the cost of sales because when it increases, it reduces a company's earnings, which in turn drive stock prices. In general, a company's sales should grow faster than its COGS.

Here is a simple example to illustrate why you have to consider the growth of COGS along with the growth in sales. Let's suppose that you run a lawn-mowing business and you rent the lawn mower each time you have a customer. You charge $50 to mow big lawns, and it costs you $10 to rent the lawnmower and to fill it with gasoline. The $50 you collect for mowing a lawn is the sales or revenue, and the $10 is the cost of sales. This means that each time you mow a lawn, you earn a profit of $40, which is calculated as the sales or revenue of $50 minus the cost of sales of $10 ($50-$10=$40). If your cost of renting the lawnmower goes up suddenly to $20, the profit for each lawn you mow will go down to $30 ($50-$20=$30) unless you raise the price you charge. You can probably raise your price a bit, but there is a limit to how much more your customers will pay for you to mow their lawns. Your customers probably won't like it if you suddenly raise your price by $10 and charge $60 to mow their lawns so that you can still maintain your $40 profit ($60-$20=$40). You can try it, but you may lose a few customers. If you raise your price by just $5 instead of $10, so that you now charge $55, you may lose fewer customers. Your profit will be $35 ($55-$20=$35) instead of the $40 you were making originally. But if expenses keep going up, there is only so much you can do to maintain a reasonable profit in your business.

Many businesses face the same dilemma of rising COGS as described in the previous example. As their COGS increase, they too have to increase their prices so that their earnings aren't significantly reduced. For many businesses, however, increasing prices to make up for higher COGS result in losing some customers. Some businesses end up compromising by raising prices somewhat (but not fully) to cover increased COGS. In the long run, the stocks of businesses whose expenses are growing faster than their revenue are not attractive investments.

Gross Profit & Gross Margin (For the Advanced Teenvestor)

The *gross profit* (also known as *gross operating profit)* is the sales less COGS. This number divided by sales is the *gross margin* (in percentage terms). The calculations are represented mathematically as follows:

Gross Profit = Sales - COGS

Gross Margin= Gross Profit x 100 / Sales

The calculations above, as with most of the calculations in this book, are simple. But it is important that you understand the information you can get out of the numbers. What gross profit tells you is how profitable the business is before taking into account the expenses not directly related to the product being sold. For example, gross profit does not consider a company's telephone expenses or rent as part of COGS. Gross profit can only tell you whether the products being sold by a company are profitable on their own. Here are the gross margins for our six sample companies:

Gross Margins					
PepsiCo (PEP)	Apple (AAPL)	McDonald's (MCD)	Merck (MRK)	Chipotle (CMG)	Alphabet (GOOG)
56%	31%	40%	63%	25%	55%

We generally prefer large-cap companies with gross margins of 35% or more, unless the company is very solid in all other ways discussed in this chapter. For mid-cap firms, we look for gross margins of more than 50% unless the companies have other strong features.

Net Profit & Profit Margin

The main reason most companies exist is to make money. *Net profit* (sometimes referred to as *net income*, *net earnings*, or just plain *earnings*) is how much profit a company makes after subtracting all its expenses. Mathematically, net profit is calculated as follows:

Net Profit = Sales - COGS - SG&A - R&D - ITDA

Where 1) COGS is cost of goods sold, 2) SG&A are selling, general and administrative expenses, 3) R&D are research and development expenses, and 4) ITDA are interest, taxes, depreciation and amortization expenses.

When all is said and done, the price of a stock increases because investors think the company will make more money in the future. When a company's net profit grows, the investor has a better chance of receiving dividends (if the company pays dividends at all), the retained earnings grow (meaning that more money is plowed back into the company), and other investors are attracted to the company because of its success (thereby driving the stock price higher).

In the world of investing, companies whose net profit grows each year in the range of 15% to 20% (or more) are considered growth stocks. For our purposes, if a company's profit has increased by 15% or more for each of the past five years, and is expected to increase by about the same amount next year, you can consider it a growth stock.

Some companies that have no earnings can still make for good investments because of the anticipation of earnings. This is the only reason the stocks of some new technology and Internet companies do well. These companies typically have losses for years as they spend a lot of money to develop their technologies. But what investors are betting on is that sometime in the future, they will start making money because of the technical superiority or the uniqueness of their products.

Once you have calculated net profit, you can then calculate *profit margin* (also known as *net margin* or *net profit margin*), which is given in percentage terms as follows:

Profit Margin = Net Profit x 100 / Sales

While net profit numbers are important, profit margins are even more significant because they can tell you how much money a company actually keeps for each dollar it gets from its customers after paying absolutely all of its expenses. Here are the profit margins for our six sample companies:

Profit Margins

PepsiCo (PEP)	Apple (AAPL)	McDonald's (MCD)	Merck (MRK)	Chipotle (CMG)	Alphabet (GOOG)
7.8%	22.6%	16.1%	24.5%	11.6%	21.8%

As with some other fundamental analysis measures, it pays to calculate net profit margin over time to see if it is steady, going down, or increasing. Ideally, you would want net profit margin to go up or stay steady. A declining profit margin is troubling unless there are some unusual circumstances that caused it. For example, when a company closes a manufacturing plant, there are usually some extra expenses associated with giving the workers *severance pay* – money workers are paid when they are fired or laid off. In the year these workers are fired or laid off, the company's expenses will increase by the severance pay. But these worker expenses will not show up on the company's income statement in the next year, so there may be no reason for alarm when the decrease in profit margin is because of such an unusual expense item. So it pays to dig deeper to find the underlying cause of a decrease in profit margin.

Some industries, such as retail clothing and consumer electronics, have low profit margins. For this reason, no one can really tell you the minimum profit margin you should seek for the company whose stock you are evaluating. What's fair to say is that if you are interested in a particular industry, choose the companies in that industry that have the highest profit margins.

Cash and Debt

A nice chunk of cash and very little debt is always good. A company with lots of cash has a good chance of surviving difficult financial times brought on by bad business conditions. In addition, the company can use the cash to expand or improve its operations when the opportunity arises. Low debt means that the company is not wasting money on interest payments.

Debt-Equity Ratio

There are simple calculations you can perform to find out about a company's debt and how much cash it can get its hands on in an emergency. One such calculation is called the *debt-equity ratio* (shown sometimes in percentage format and sometimes in decimal format). One common type of debt-equity ratio is the ratio of total debt to equity (or common stock or shareholder's equity). A company's total debt can be found in the liability section of its balance sheet. The equity, which represents the investments in the company by its owners, can usually be found near the end of a company's balance sheet. The mathematical representation of the debt-equity ratio when shown in decimal format is:

Debt-Equity Ratio = Total Debt / Equity

When represented in percentage format, the debt-equity ratio is calculated as follows:

Debt-Equity Ratio = Total Debt x 100 / Equity

The higher the debt-equity ratio, the more money the company has borrowed. And of course, the higher the borrowed amount, the higher the interest payment, which is really just another expense, as we explained earlier.

If you recall our SportsTee example in Chapter 3, the partners of the company contributed a total of $2,500 (the equity) and borrowed $1,000. For SportsTee, the debt-equity ratio was $1000/$2500 = 0.40 or 40%.

There is no single debt-equity ratio benchmark that is appropriate for all industries. Some industries are known for borrowing more money than others. Construction and telecommunications industries are great examples of industries that traditionally carry lots of debt. It is best to compare debt-equity ratios of companies in the same industries and to look at the trends of the ratio as well. If you find that the company in which you want to invest belongs to an industry that normally has a high debt-equity ratio, make sure that company has one of the lowest debt-equity ratios in that industry group.

Here are the debt-equity ratios for our six sample companies:

Debt-Equity Ratio

PepsiCo (PEP)	Apple (AAPL)	McDonald's (MCD)	Merck (MRK)	Chipotle (CMG)	Alphabet (GOOG)
2.37	0.43	1.70	0.57	N/A*	.071

*Company Had No Debt

In addition to looking at the current debt-equity ratio, it is also good to look at how this ratio changes over time. Compare the debt-equity ratios for the company over a 5-year period. In general, a falling debt-equity ratio means the company is paying off some of the loans it has taken out. This is usually good news for people who want to invest in the company.

Current Ratio

Another measurement that can tell you whether a company will be able to pay what it owes is the current ratio which we covered in Chapter 5 in the context of the SportsTee balance sheet. To calculate the current ratio, you need the current asset and the current liability of a balance sheet. Just to refresh your memory, a current asset is an asset that is due the company within one year. For example, the current asset on a company's balance sheet could be its certificates of deposit, or CDs – a short-term loan to a bank. Current liabilities are liabilities due in less than one year. Examples could be a loan the company takes out that is due in three months. The current ratio, which is usually shown in decimal format, is current assets divided by current liabilities. The calculation is as follows:

Current Ratio = Current Assets / Current Liabilities

In general, the higher the current ratio, the better off the company, because it indicates that the company can afford to pay its immediate bills. For example, a current ratio of 2 is better than a current ratio of 1. Once again, look at the current ratio of other companies in the same industry as the company you are investigating. If the current ratio is around the same level as the other companies, you are probably in good shape.

In addition, look at the growth or decrease in the current ratio. A steady decrease in the current ratio over the past three to five years could spell trouble. Here are the current ratios for our six sample companies:

Current Ratios

PepsiCo (PEP)	Apple (AAPL)	McDonald's (MCD)	Merck (MRK)	Chipotle (CMG)	Alphabet (GOOG)
1.20	1.09	2.16	1.62	3.79	4.85

Think for a minute about what these numbers mean. Merck's current ratio of 1.62, for example, means that it has 1.62 times the short-term assets it needs to pay off any debt that will come due in the next one to 12 months.

Return on Equity

Return on equity (ROE) is the best way to learn how much money a company is making for its investors. It is calculated by dividing the company's net profit by its equity. It is represented mathematically (in percentage terms) as follows:

$$ROE = Net\ Profit \times 100\ /\ Equity$$

ROE can reveal how much money the company is making compared with how much it has invested to make that money. Just to use a simple example, if you invest $100 in a rare baseball card and sell it for $120, your net profit will be $20 ($120 - $100 = $20), and your ROE would be $20/$100 or 20%. The $100 in the denominator is your equity in the card business. The 20% ROE represents your percentage return on that $100 investment. The ROE is the same as the "return on investment" concept we discussed in Chapter 10, since "investment" is really just another term for equity. Here are the ROEs for our six sample companies:

Return On Equity (ROE)

PepsiCo (PEP)	Apple (AAPL)	McDonald's (MCD)	Merck (MRK)	Chipotle (CMG)	Alphabet (GOOG)
27.71%	41.15%	31.29%	20.63%	25.71%	13.86%

When looking at a company, it is important to look at the trend in ROE to make sure that it is not steadily declining. Experienced investors sometimes look at the ROE of other companies in the same industry to make sure that the company they are looking at is performing in line with its competitors.

In Chapter 10, we discussed one of the basic investment strategies many investors use in choosing stock: value investing. Value investors tend to look for bargains in the stock market. That is, they look for companies that are temporarily doing poorly or not living up to their promise, but give reason to hope that they will soon become more profitable. One of the ways value investors determine whether a stock's poor performance is temporary is to look carefully at its historical ROEs. The logic goes something like this: if the average ROE in the past five years has been 20% and the ROE for the last year was 10%, there is a good chance the ROE may get back to its old 20% level eventually. For a long-term investor this logic may work, but it may not work for a short-term investor (which we hope you are not).

Earnings per Share

Earnings per share, or EPS, is the amount of money the company actually earns for each share of stock held by investors. It is calculated, in dollars per share, as follows:

EPS = Net Profit / (#Of Common Shares Outstanding)

Ideally, EPS should increase each year. Here are the EPS figures for our six sample companies available at the time of this writing:

Earnings Per Share (EPS)					
PepsiCo (PEP)	Apple (AAPL)	McDonald's (MCD)	Merck (MRK)	Chipotle (CMG)	Alphabet (GOOG)
3.37	8.65	4.30	3.42	16.33	21.22

As discussed earlier, companies report their earnings for each quarter – in other words, every three months. Just before companies announce their quarterly earnings to the world, investment analysts make predictions about these companies' EPS for the current quarter and for the year (or years) to come. This information can give you a good idea about what the best minds on Wall Street think of certain companies.

Wall Street analysts publish their best EPS estimates for big, publicly traded companies. When these companies finally report their earnings, most investors compare the Wall Street analysts' projections with the companies' actual EPS figures for the quarter. If actual EPS figures are more than the Wall Street analysts' projections, even by 10 cents a share, the stock prices of the companies usually go up. Stock prices can also go down when actual EPS figures are less than the predicted amounts.

Teenvestors are surprised when they find out that even small differences between predicted and actual EPS numbers can influence companies' stock prices. To make sense of it, they have to consider what the differences say about the profitability of these companies. For example, PepsiCo has about 1.44 billion shares in the hands of investors. If the company's EPS is 10 cents less than predicted by analysts, it means that its earnings were about $144 million (10 cents x 1.44 billion shares = $144 million) less than was expected – a big number even for a company like PepsiCo. As you can see, this EPS difference makes a clear statement that the company is not making as much money as was predicted. And because expectations can affect stock prices (as we discussed in Chapter 9), any difference between expectations and reality is likely to affect the price of any stock.

We recommend that Teenvestors ignore analysts' EPS projections for the current quarter and focus on long-term projections and the reasons for them. What should matter to you is what the analysts feel the stock will do in the next year or two. See if their logic makes sense to you; invest for the future, not the present.

Price-Earnings Ratio

The *price-earnings ratio*, or PE (also known as PE ratio), is one of those topics that we have to discuss, not because it is so important to Teenvestors, but because a lot of other investors focus on it. The PE is one way investors determine how much a stock costs compared with how much profit the company makes. The PE is today's price of the stock divided by the EPS of the company over the past year. Mathematically, it is calculated as follows:

$$PE = \text{Today's Price Per Share} / EPS$$

Like most of the data in this chapter, PE ratios can be found on a number of good financial websites. The way to interpret PE is that it tells you how many years it will take for you to get back your investment if you buy one share of a company's stock (and all of the company's net profit each year gets distributed as dividends). By way of example, suppose you buy a share of Teenvestor Inc. at $30 and the yearly EPS (earnings per share) is $2. This means that the first year after buying the stock, you would earn $2. You'd earn another $2 for the second year; and another $2 for the third year. If we keep going, you will see that it would take 15 years to earn back a total of $30 – your initial investment. You could have figured out how long it would take to earn back the $30 investment by dividing the stock price by the earnings per share ($30/$2 = 15).

Investors refer to stock as either cheap or expensive based on PE levels. For a given stock, a PE of, say, 20 is more expensive than a PE of 15. Some value investors believe that over a long period of time, the PE ratios of companies stay stable, so they watch PEs to see when it is cheap for them to buy the stock. For example, if the PE ratio of Teenvestor Inc. has been 50 for the past 10 years, and is suddenly 30, these value investors will buy more of Teenvestor Inc.'s stock in hopes that the PE ratio will move back up to 50, meaning that the stock price may go back up. But one major flaw in focusing solely on PE ratios is that they can increase even if a stock's price does not change very much. If EPS goes down, the PE ratio can go up. What this means is that if you buy Teenvestor Inc.'s stock when it has a PE ratio of 30, and it later goes to a PE ratio of 50, it would not necessarily mean that the company's stock price went up. It could mean that earnings per share went down, without an equivalent change in the value of the stock. Still, a PE ratio can serve as a general guide as to whether a stock is more expensive or cheaper relative to its earnings.

Growth stocks (or companies whose earnings grow by 15% to 20% or more per year over several years) usually have high PE ratios. These ratios are typically high for technology and Internet companies, if they make money at all. For example, at the height of the Internet boom in 2000, the PE ratio for eBay, the online auction house, was over 2300 (as opposed to a PE ratio of around 15 in 2015). The high level of the PE ratio at that time was not really meaningful to investors, since it was so big only because eBay was making very little money at that time. In other words, eBay's tiny earnings at that time, used in the denominator of the PE formula (Price Per Share / Earnings Per Share), made the ratio very big. To drive the point home, what will be the PE ratio of a company that has no earnings? Mathematically, when you divide any stock price by 0 (which represents no earnings), you will get an infinite number. Of course, an infinite PE ratio is meaningless. For new industries (such as those created from the Internet), you can't use the PE ratio as a measure of whether companies are cheap or expensive until these companies have had positive earnings over a 3- to 5-year period. And even then, using PE ratios as the only way to spot bargains in technology stocks is flawed. Here are the PE ratios for our six sample companies available at the time of this writing:

Price Earnings Ratio (PE Ratio)					
PepsiCo (PEP)	Apple (AAPL)	McDonald's (MCD)	Merck (MRK)	Chipotle (CMG)	Alphabet (GOOG)
30.39	13.16	24.16	14.78	39.79	33.08

SETTING UP A DUMMY PORTFOLIO

Setting up a dummy portfolio is one way Teenvestors can overcome the fear of taking that first step in investing. Portfolios set up on these websites get recalculated regularly to tell you exactly how much you have made or lost on your investments. For nearly all these websites, you have to register (for free) in order to use their portfolio services.

You can begin by setting up two different portfolios – one made up of small cap stocks and another made up of large cap stocks. Keep the stocks in these portfolios constant for a few months and track the movements of the two portfolios to understand how size can make a big difference in how quickly stocks move up and down. If there are any unusual price movements in the individual stocks in your portfolio, scan the news to see if these movements can be explained by current events or any news about the companies experiencing volatile stock prices.

Some of the websites with tools for setting up dummy portfolios inculde: Yahoo!Finance, Investopedia, Google Finance, Morningstar, and many others.

For more information, website links, videos, and any assignments associated with this chapter, please visit:

www.teenvestor.com/chapter13

14

UNDERSTANDING MUTUAL FUNDS

Let's suppose that you have $500 to invest in the stock market. However, you are concerned that you might lose too much of your money if you put it all in the stock of one company. So, you decide that you would like to spread your investment into several companies. In other words, you want to diversify your investment as we described in Chapter 10. Of course, to diversify your investments, you have to put your money in the shares of companies in different industries so that if the shares of one company you invest in go down, other companies whose shares you are holding may be able to make up for this decrease if they go up in value.

Because $500 is not really enough money with which to diversify your investment, you find three other friends who have $500 each and pool your combined $2,000 ($500 from you and a total of $1,500 from your other three friends). With the $2,000, you purchase about $500 worth of stock in each of four companies in different industries, such as the pharmaceutical, banking, computer and automobile industries. Each of the four people who contributed to the pool of $2,000 owns 25% of the investments you have made with the money. This means that each person owns 25% of the dividends and 25% of the capital appreciation (or the increase in the value of the stock). When the investments are *liquidated* – that is, when the shares are sold – each person who contributed gets 25% of the amount for which you sell the shares.

The collective investment you have made with the $2,000 pool of cash is really a *mutual fund*. This chapter explains the basics of mutual fund investing: how a mutual fund works, what factors to consider before investing, and how to avoid common pitfalls.

GENERAL INFORMATION ABOUT MUTUAL FUNDS

A mutual fund is a company that brings together money from many people and invests it in stocks, bonds, or other financial assets (or *securities*, as they are collectively known). These combined holdings of the fund are known as its *portfolio*. Each investor owns shares, which represent a portion of each of the securities in the portfolio. In the example of your investment of $2,000 in the stocks of companies in four industries, each investor owned one-quarter of the investment.

There are many different types of funds. There are funds that invest in technology, foreign, small-cap or any other variety of stocks you can think of. What all funds have in common is that they need *portfolio managers*. These managers are responsible for buying stocks and other securities for mutual funds. They are also responsible for selling and substituting securities in the fund. Professional management of mutual funds is the main reason a lot of investors buy mutual funds in the first place. These investors feel that they just don't have the time or the skill to determine which stocks to buy on their own.

Mutual funds have their own symbols just like stocks. A mutual fund can own as few as 20 different stocks or as many as 500. There is no limit to the market value of the stocks in mutual funds. At the time of this writing, one of the biggest mutual funds, Vanguard Total Stock Market Idx I (symbol: VITSX) had assets worth nearly $400 billion. This number changes depending on what is happening in the economy. More people put money in mutual funds during a bull market, and they move their money to safer investments when the economy is doing poorly.

Mutual funds usually publish the amount of money they make for investors each year as they seek to attract more investors. The amount they make for the investors is called the fund's *annualized total return*. Funds often publish their 1-year, 3-year, 5-year, and 10-year annualized total returns to boast about how much they have increased investors' money. This figure is usually given in percentage terms. Even though most funds only publish average returns over specified periods, the yearly returns are probably the best way to see how much the fund's returns move up or down.

Advertisements, rankings, and ratings tell you how well a fund has performed in the past. The more you study mutual funds, however, the more you will realize that a fund's past performance is not as important as you might think. Studies show that future returns can be quite different from historical returns. This year's "number one" fund can easily become next year's below-average fund.

WHY MUTUAL FUNDS ARE NOT ALWAYS TEENVESTOR-FRIENDLY

We want to tell you from the outset that we don't consider most mutual funds very Teenvestor-friendly. For one thing, many mutual funds require initial investments that range from $1,000 to $3,000. There are a few funds, however, that require as little as a $100 initial investment, as long as the investor puts in the same amount monthly until a target total investment amount is reached. But how many Teenvestors really have that kind of cash on hand every month?

Another reason we don't think mutual funds are always Teenvestor-friendly is that figuring out how much tax you owe on the money you make with your mutual fund investments can be complicated. If you own many varieties of mutual funds and you buy and sell shares frequently, you and your parents will probably have to consult an accountant.

Despite our opinion about the problems of Teenvestors investing in mutual funds, we feel that we should still cover how to go about choosing funds, just in case you have the cash to do it and you can get help to fill out your tax forms (if you buy and sell shares frequently). If you *do* choose to invest in mutual funds, you should stick to those funds that invest in stocks since, as we discussed earlier, stocks generally can make more money for you over a long time. In the website link associated with this chapter, you will find a list of some Teenvestor-friendly mutual funds.

THE ADVANTAGES OF MUTUAL FUNDS

Mutual funds can be a good way for Teenvestors to invest in stocks and bonds (if they can overcome the obstacles mentioned above) for the following reasons:

1. Mutual funds are run by professional money managers.

2. By owning shares in a mutual fund instead of buying individual stocks or bonds directly, you spread out your investment risk.

3. Because a mutual fund buys and sells large amounts of stocks and bonds (and other financial assets) at a time, its costs are often lower than what you would pay on your own.

NET ASSET VALUE

When we speak of the value of a share of stock, we say that it is worth a specific dollar amount. The value of a share in a mutual fund is referred to as its Net Asset Value per share, or NAV. When you buy mutual fund shares, you pay the current NAV per share, plus any sales charge (also called a *sales load*). When you sell your shares, the fund will pay you the total NAV value at the time of the sale, less any other sales load. A fund's NAV goes up or down daily as the values of the individual stocks in the fund change.

As an example, suppose you invest $1,000 in a mutual fund with a NAV of $10. You will therefore own 100 shares of the fund. If, after you make your investment, the NAV of the mutual fund drops to $9 (because the value of the fund's portfolio has dropped), you will still own 100 shares, but your investment will be worth $900. If after you make your investment, the NAV goes up to $11, your investment will be worth $1,100. This example assumes no sales charge.

KINDS OF MUTUAL FUNDS

You take risks when you invest in any mutual fund. You may lose some or all of the money you invest (your principal) because the value of the stocks (or securities) held by a fund goes up and down.

Each kind of mutual fund has different risks. Generally, the higher the potential return (the money you can make), the higher the risk of loss.

Before you invest, decide whether the goals and risks of any fund you are considering are a good fit for you. To make this decision, you may need the help of a financial adviser. There are also investment books and services to guide you.

The three main categories of mutual funds are money market funds, bond funds, and stock funds. There are a variety of types within each category.

Money Market Funds

Money market funds have relatively low risks compared with other mutual funds. They are limited by law to certain high-quality, short-term investments. Money market funds try to keep their value (NAV) at a stable $1.00 per share, but NAV may fall below $1.00 if their investments perform poorly. Investor losses on money market funds have been rare, but they are possible. Losses occurred with one money market fund during the financial crisis in 2008 commonly referred to as the "Great Recession." Investors typically earn a relatively low interest rate or "yield" on their shares.

Bond Funds

Bond funds (also called *fixed income funds*) have higher risks than money market funds, but they seek to pay higher returns. Unlike money market funds, bond funds are not restricted to high-quality or short-term investments. Because there are many different types of bonds, bond funds can vary dramatically in their risks.

Most bond funds have credit risk, which is the risk that companies or other issuers whose bonds are owned by the fund may fail to pay their debts (including the debt owed to holders of their bonds). Some funds have little credit risk, such as those that invest in government bonds. But be careful: nearly all bond funds have interest-rate risk, which means that the value of the bonds they hold will go down when interest rates go up. Because of this, you can lose money in any bond fund, including those that invest only in government bonds.

Long-term bond funds invest in bonds with longer *maturities* (length of time until the final payout). The values (NAVs) of long-term bond funds can go up or down more rapidly than those of short-term bond funds.

Stock Funds

Stock funds (also called *equity funds*) generally involve more risk than money market or bond funds, but they also can offer the highest returns (or the highest profit). A stock fund's value (NAV) can rise and fall quickly over the short term, but historically stocks have performed better over the long term than other types of investments.

Not all stock funds are the same. For example, *growth* funds focus on stocks that may not pay a regular dividend but have the potential to increase in value. *Income* funds invest in stocks that pay regular dividends. *Index* funds aim to offer the same returns as specific market indices such as the S&P 500 Index by investing in all – or perhaps a representative sample – of the companies included in the index. *Sector* funds specialize in a particular industry segment such as technology or consumer products stocks.

Stock funds are more appropriate for Teenvestors than bond funds.

THE THREE WAYS YOU CAN EARN MONEY WITH FUNDS

You can earn money from your mutual fund investment in three ways. First, a fund may receive income in the form of dividends and interest on the securities it owns. A fund will pay its shareholders nearly all of the income it has earned in the form of *dividends*.

Second, the price of the securities a fund owns may increase – this is known as *capital appreciation*, as explained in Chapter 10. When a fund sells a security that has increased in price, the fund has a *capital gain*. At the end of the year, most funds distribute these capital gains to investors.

Third, if a fund does not sell but instead holds on to securities that have increased in price, the value of its shares (NAV) increases. The higher NAV reflects the higher value of your investment. If you sell your shares, you make a profit (and this is also a capital gain).

Usually funds will give you a choice: the fund can send you the *distributions* (capital gains and dividends), or you can have them *reinvested* in the fund to buy more shares, often without paying an additional sales load.

GETTING INFORMATION ON MUTUAL FUNDS

There are sources of information that you should consult before you invest in mutual funds. The most important of these is the fund's *prospectus*. The *prospectus* is the fund's selling document and contains information about costs, risks, past performance, and the fund's investment goals. You should be able to obtain a full prospectus or a summary of one online, from a financial investment professional if you are using one, or by mail from the fund itself.

Read the fund's prospectus before you invest. Check its *annualized total returns* (sometimes called just "total returns" in the prospectus). You will find it in the Financial Highlights, near the front of the prospectus.

Observe how total return has varied over the years. The Financial Highlights in the prospectus show yearly total return for the most recent 10-year period. An impressive 10-year total return may be based on one spectacular year followed by many average years.

Looking at year-to-year changes in total return is a good way to see how stable the fund's returns have been.

THINGS TO CONSIDER WHEN CHOOSING AND INVESTING IN A FUND

You can buy some mutual funds by contacting them directly. Others are sold mainly through brokers, banks, financial planners, or insurance agents. All mutual funds will *redeem* (or buy back) your shares on any business day and must send you the payment within seven days. Just as with stocks, however, you can't buy mutual funds unless you are at least 18 years old. Your parents have to establish a special account called a *custodial account* for you to buy any mutual funds. See Chapter 22 for more information on custodial accounts.

Even though we don't think most mutual funds are very Teenvestor-friendly, the following sections will help to point you to the right type of funds in which to invest while staying away from the funds that are too risky.

Stick With a Simple Strategy

Teenvestors should not invest in funds they don't really understand. The following suggestions should help you keep things simple.

Index Funds

A lot of mutual funds spend a lot of time and money trying to choose the right stocks for their portfolios. Fund managers choose stocks that they think will go up in price and dump stocks that they think will go down in price. These types of funds are called *actively managed* funds because someone actually has to watch the fund carefully to determine whether to buy or sell the fund's assets. These actively managed funds charge investors a lot of money for their efforts in trying to increase the funds' value. But what many investors don't know is that there are mutual funds that need no managers, and yet do very well. These types of funds are called *index funds*. The most common index funds are made up of stocks in the S&P 500. (Recall that the stocks in the S&P 500 are 500 of the biggest companies in the country.) Another common index fund is one that mirrors the Wilshire 5000, an index that reflects the U.S. stock market.

Index funds made up of the S&P 500 stocks generally perform better than most stock funds. When you stop to think about it, this is really shocking. What this says is that a mutual fund that simply holds S&P 500 stocks does better on the average than most funds that are actively managed by hot-shot Wall Street geniuses. There is no guarantee, however, that such index funds will continue to do better than nearly all stock funds that are actively managed. Nevertheless, index funds are an easy choice for Teenvestors who don't want to knock themselves out choosing funds out of the thousands available.

Teenvestors should try index funds, at least when they start investing in mutual funds. You can find index funds through the links at the end of this chapter.

Getting Information on Funds

The best way to begin investigating an index fund (indeed, any fund) is to use the Internet for more information. Like stocks, mutual funds also have their own symbols so you can look them up easily on websites that specialize in financial data. We find Yahoo!Finance and Marketwatch helpful in gathering information on specific mutual funds.

Costs of Investing in a Mutual Fund

When you buy a mutual fund, you have to pay an up-front fee and then an ongoing fee for as long as you own the fund. You can find the estimate for a fund's fees in the *fee table* near the front of the fund's prospectus. You can use the fee table to compare the costs of different funds. The table breaks costs into two main categories: *sales loads* (paid when you buy, sell, or exchange your shares) and *expense ratios* (or yearly ongoing expenses).

Sales Loads

A *sales load* is a term you should become familiar with if you intend to invest in mutual funds. A mutual fund charges a sales load to pay commissions to the people who sell the fund's shares to investors, as well as to pay other marketing costs. Loads, which are usually given in percentage terms, can be as high as 6% of your investment. That is, if you invest $100 into buying a share of a mutual fund, $6 will be taken out to pay commission.

Some funds require you to pay the load when you buy shares. This is known as paying a *front-end load*. Others require that you pay when you sell your shares. This is known as paying a *back-end load*. Some funds charge no loads at all, and these are known as *no-load funds*.

Of course, the bad thing about a front-end load is that it eats your money away immediately as soon as you invest in the fund. This may not be so bad if the value of your investment is going to skyrocket, but the best way for Teenvestors to avoid these charges is to stick to no-load funds.

Expense Ratio

Regardless of whether a fund has a load or not, funds charge investors each year primarily for managing the investments. Remember that in a mutual fund, you leave the people managing the fund in charge of determining what stocks to buy and sell. The manager of course is paid handsomely for his or her efforts. The cost of running the fund also includes things as basic as printing and postage associated with the statements mailed to fund owners. Finally, funds also charge investors what's known as *12b-1 fees* – marketing and distribution fees. All of these costs are lumped into what is called the *expense ratio*, which is the percentage of the value of your investment that will go toward paying these costs for each year the investor owns the fund.

Some investors mistakenly believe that if the expense ratios of their funds are high, the managers of the funds must be really good. The truth is that funds with high expense ratios do not typically perform better than those with low expense ratios. But there may be circumstances in which you decide it is appropriate for you to pay higher expenses. For example, you can expect to pay higher expenses for certain types of funds that require extra work by their managers, such as international stock funds, which call for more sophisticated research. You may also pay higher expenses for funds that provide special services, such as telephone support, check-writing and automatic investment programs.

A difference in expenses that may look small to you can make a big difference in the value of your investment over time. In other words, the higher the expense ratio, the lower your return will be, especially if you hang on to a mutual fund for a long time. We recommend that before you buy a mutual fund, you find out from the prospectus the estimates for the expenses it will charge. The prospectus should lay all these expenses out in detail.

TAXES

You may owe taxes on any year you receive or reinvest distributions from your mutual fund. You may also owe taxes on any capital gains you receive when you sell your shares. Just as with stocks, you have to *keep your account statements to figure out your taxes at the end of the year.* If you invest in a *tax-exempt fund* (such as a municipal bond fund), some or all of your dividends will be exempt from federal (and sometimes state and local) income tax. You may, however, owe taxes on any capital gains.

> For more information, website links, videos, and any assignments associated with this chapter, please visit:
>
> www.teenvestor.com/chapter14

15

EXCHANGE TRADED FUNDS

Exchange traded funds (ETFs) are investments that have characteristics of both stocks and mutual funds. To review for a moment, a stock is an ownership interest in a company. It is traded on a national stock exchange, and the price can change from minute to minute. By contrast, a mutual fund share is an ownership interest in a diversified basket of stocks, and the price (or NAV) of one share of the fund (at least for open-end funds) is generally calculated once a day. To sell or buy mutual funds, you'd generally have to wait until 4 P.M. on the day of your transaction to get the value of the shares you are selling or buying.

Another difference between stocks and mutual funds, as far as Teenvestors are concerned, is that it takes a lot more money to invest in mutual funds than in stocks. As we explained in another chapter, the minimum balance for the listed no-load index funds is generally about $2,500 or more. This is still a lot of money for young or first-time investors. Stocks, on the other hand, can be purchased for about the price quoted when you trade, without any minimum purchase requirements.

DEFINING AN ETF

ETFs, also called *index shares*, are investments that represent a diversified group of companies (just like mutual funds) but trade like stocks. They've been around since about 1993, which is a short time for an investment product. At that time there were close to 120 stock-based ETFs in the market and just a handful of bond-based ETFs. There are now more than 1,500 ETFs that cover a variety of indices and sectors.

Most ETFs trading in the marketplace are index-based. These ETFs seek to deliver the same return as an index like the S&P 500, and they generally invest primarily in the component securities of the index. For example, the SPDR, or "spider" ETF, which seeks to track the S&P 500, invests in most or all of the equity securities contained in that index. Some but not all ETFs may post their holdings on their websites on a daily basis.

Increasingly, ETFs are based on indexes that are designed to track specific market sectors such as mining, petroleum, and gaming. Thus, an ETF may be based on an index specifically designed to meet the ETF sponsor's customers' interests. Generally, some information about the index (including, for some, the methodology used to determine what securities will be included in the index) is available, but the specific component securities making up the index may or may not be.

Actively managed ETFs are not based on an index. Instead, they seek to achieve a stated investment objective by investing in a portfolio of stocks, bonds, and other assets. Unlike with an index-

TABLE 15.1			
Major Index-Based Exchange Traded Funds			
ETF	Index Tracked	Symbol	Website
SPDR S&P 500	US large- and midcap stocks selected by the S&P Committee.	SPY	www.spdrindex.com
iShares Core S&P 500	US large- and midcap stocks selected by the S&P Committee.	IVV	www.ishares.com
iShares MSCI EAFE	Developed-market securities based in Europe, Australia and the Far East	EFA	www.ishares.com
Vanguard Total Stock Market	US equities market, encompassing the entire market-cap spectrum.	VTI	www.vanguard.com
Vanguard FTSE Emerging Markets	Emerging markets stocks, excluding South Korea.	VWO	www.vanguard.com
PowerShares QQQ	100 NASDAQ-listed stocks.	QQQ	www.nasdaq.com
Vanguard S&P 500	U.S. large- and midcap stocks selected by the S&P Committee.	VOO	www.vanguard.com
iShares Russell 2000	US small-cap stocks. The index selects stocks ranked 1,001-3,000 by market cap.	IWN	www.ishares.com
iShares Russell 1000 Growth	US large- and midcap stocks selected from the Russell 1000 Index with the highest growth characteristics.	IWF	www.ishares.com
iShares MSCI Emerging Markets	Emerging markets firms weighted by market cap.	EEM	www.ishares.com

based ETF, an adviser of an actively managed ETF may actively buy or sell components in the portfolio on a daily basis without regard to conformity with an index. Actively managed ETFs are required to publish their holdings daily.

ETFs AND THE SMALL INVESTOR

ETFs have several advantages that make them suitable for Teenvestors and other small investors:

1. They are a good way to hold diversified stocks without having to diversify on your own.
2. They generally charge lower annual expense ratios than mutual funds.
3. They have lower capital gains taxes, as the funds generally do not do much trading and therefore capital gains are minimal.
4. They have all-day tracking and trading.
5. Their initial investment amount can be less than $100, as opposed to an index mutual fund's investment minimum that's generally around $2,500.

BUYING ETFs

Buying ETFs is as easy as buying stocks from your online broker. The only difference is that with ETFs, there is a prospectus available to help you understand the fund's investment strategy. You should make absolutely sure that you are investing in the ETF of the index you'd like to hold, such as the S&P 500 or the NASDAQ. Any of the websites that can give you a stock quote can provide you with the information you need about your ETF of choice. Our first stop is usually www.etf.com, but you can try the other research websites we listed in the chapter link, www.teenvestor.com/chapter15. Type in the symbol for the ETF you are interested in researching, and you will get information on the fund's profile. Table 15.1 shows some of the biggest index ETFs in the market.

For more information, website links, videos, and any assignments associated with this chapter, please visit:

www.teenvestor.com/chapter15

TeenVestor

16

BUYING STOCKS DIRECTLY FROM COMPANIES

Did you know that you could buy stock directly from public companies without going through a broker? In this chapter, you will learn about the two ways public companies allow you to buy their stock directly from them: through direct purchase plans and dividend reinvestment plans (DRIPs). You will learn how these plans work, the major difference between the two, and how to use these investment plans effectively so you can get the most for your investment dollar.

WHY COMPANIES OFFER DIRECT PURCHASE PLANS AND DRIPS

You may wonder why companies would want to encourage small-time investors to buy their stock by offering direct purchase plans and DRIPs. The answer is quite simple: companies that offer some form of stock purchase plans see them as a way to encourage an investor to become a loyal customer. For example, if you own shares in McDonald's, chances are that you would rather buy McDonald's food than Burger King's (assuming you occasionally eat fast food). In addition, direct purchase plans give companies a cheap way to raise money directly from investors rather than going through investment bankers who would underwrite stock offerings. More than 1,600 companies now have some form of a stock purchase program.

THE DIFFERENCE BETWEEN DIRECT PURCHASE PLANS AND DRIPS

Direct Purchase Plans

Companies that allow you *to economically purchase your first share*, and all other shares, of their stock directly from them without going through a broker are said to have direct purchase plans. These shares are also called *no-load-stock* or *no-load-shares*, because you can purchase them without a broker's fee or *load* (although you may be charged a small administrative fee).

More than 400 companies currently offer direct purchase plans, and the number is growing each year.

At least 22 companies in the Dow currently offer direct purchase plans. Some of these companies, which you might recognize, are: Walt Disney Co., Exxon Mobil Corp., Nike Inc., and McDonald's Corp.

Dividend Reinvestment Plans (DRIPs)

Companies that allow you to buy additional shares of their stock directly if you already own one or more shares of the company's stock are said to have dividend reinvestment plans (DRIPs).

You will find that some investors use the terms "direct purchase plans" and "DRIPs" interchangeably, but there really is a difference between the two. This difference can be significant to Teenvestors, who have little money to invest in the first place. Historically, the most significant difference between direct purchase plans and DRIPs is that a company that offers only a DRIP will generally not allow you to purchase your first share from it directly (unless you spend a ridiculous amount of money for the initial purchase). Unless you already own a share of that company and it is registered in your name, you would have to purchase your first share of the company's stock through a broker. Of course, once you have that initial share, you're set. You can then participate in the DRIP and take advantage of the reduced fees offered through it. Companies such as Boeing and Travelers offer only DRIPs. The "dividend reinvestment" part of these plans refers to the fact that when you participate in them, your dividends are automatically reinvested in additional shares of the company's stock.

THE STOCK REGISTRATION REQUIREMENT

Both direct purchase plans and DRIPs require that all shares you buy as a participant in the plans be registered in your name. Usually, when a stockbroker buys shares for you, the stocks are registered in the name of the firm for which the broker works (or in the *street name*, as it is called). For example, if you buy one share of Nike's stock through a broker, the share belongs to you but Nike does not have any idea that you actually own it. All Nike knows is that your broker has one share that belongs to someone. To participate in

DRIPs, however, the company whose stock you own must be aware that you personally own one of their shares. To accomplish this, your broker must buy your initial share, register the security in your name, and have the stock certificate mailed to you. All brokers (new online brokers as well as traditional brokers) can do this effortlessly. The certificate is the proof that companies with stock investment plans need to allow you to participate.

Some brokerage firms charge ridiculously high fees for transferring the security in your name. Others charge more affordable fees for this transfer. After the transfer, the company whose stock you own will recognize you as a shareholder, and it will send annual reports and other investment material directly to you. More important, you will then qualify for the company's DRIP if it has one.

THE RIGHT PLANS FOR TEENVESTORS

Over the years, the practical differences between direct purchase plans and DRIPs have narrowed because companies that offer DRIPs have administrators who can facilitate the process of your purchase of your first share. Ultimately, no matter whether you invest through a direct purchase plan or a DRIP, all that should matter to you is how much money you have to put upfront and how much additional money, if any, you are required to contribute to the plan. Overall, Teenvestors will generally find direct purchase plans more affordable than DRIPs. Companies that have direct purchase plans usually have smaller initial or enrollment fees, which will then allow investors to continue to buy additional shares.

In general, the major advantages of direct purchase plans and DRIPs are as follows:

1. *Both Encourage Teenvestors to Get Into the Market.* When a Teenvestor finds a good, stable company with strong growth potential, she can start a small portfolio and build it over time. Take Exxon Mobil Corp. for instance. The company requires that you make an initial investment of $250 in its DRIP. Another company, Kellogg's, requires an initial investment of $50. On the higher end of the initial investment scale, McDonald's has a minimum initial investment of $500, but for a custodial account (which would be the account for most Teenvestors), it is only $100.

2. *Both Allow Optional Cash Investments.* That is, they allow you to buy additional shares periodically. While the initial investment amount for ExxonMobil is $250, the additional optional monthly investment is $50 for no additional fee. For Kellogg's, which has an initial investment requirement of $50, the additional optional monthly investment is $25 or more for no additional fee. McDonald's has a minimum initial investment of $500 ($100 for custodial accounts) but an optional additional investment of $50 or more. Since the initial and optional share purchases are in dollar amounts, a Teenvestor is actually buying fractions of shares for his contributions. For example, if the stock price of a company is currently $100 per share and a Teenvestor contributes $25 to

buy additional shares in the company's DRIP, the Teenvestor would own an additional one-quarter of a share ($25/$100 = ¼).

3. *Both Charge Very Little in Brokerage Fees.* The companies save investors brokerage fees by pooling the money of the various investors before approaching brokers to buy the shares or sell them on your behalf. This way, the fees are effectively reduced for each investor. When you want to sell shares, the fees are also very low due to the pooling of all sellers.

4. *Both Plans Permit Dividend Reinvestment.* This is great for Teenvestors because the dividends they will be getting on just a few shares of stock would not amount to much. It is, therefore, better to just keep it all in the till to buy additional shares.

DISADVANTAGES OF DIRECT PURCHASE PLANS AND DRIPS

The disadvantages of direct purchase plans and DRIPs relate to taxes and the ability to buy or sell shares quickly.

With regard to taxes, you have to be organized enough to keep accurate records about the amount and the timing of your purchases and of your reinvested dividends. Even if a company does not distribute dividends to you and just reinvests those dividends to buy more shares for you, you will still owe taxes on the reinvestment amount. We won't go through the specifics of the tax issues here, but you should understand that you have to keep proper records about the activities in your account to make it easier for either your parents or an accountant to help you with taxes.

Another disadvantage of direct purchase plans and DRIPs is that they are not for people who want to trade in and out of stocks quickly. For one thing, companies that offer such plans do not offer you the ability to buy or sell stocks whenever you would like. Some of these companies may buy or sell additional shares for their DRIP investors weekly, monthly, or even quarterly. This means that you may miss out on short-term movements of stock prices. This is not really a disadvantage for Teenvestors, since their investment goals should be for gains over the long term. If you do your research, you are likely to find companies that fit those goals.

> For more information, website links, videos, and any assignments associated with this chapter, please visit:
>
> www.teenvestor.com/chapter16

TeenVestor

17

OTHER INVESTMENTS

Even though the stock market is the best place to invest your money, there are a few other financial assets you can buy. Certificates of Deposit and U.S. Savings Bonds are just two examples of other investments Teenvestors can afford with their small budgets. These two financial assets both behave like bonds because they both pay interest on invested amounts that are typically higher than any interest you will get in a regular savings account in a bank.

CERTIFICATES OF DEPOSIT

Certificates of deposit, or CDs as they are commonly known, are small loans investors make to banks for a few months to several years. The amount of money loaned is usually called the *principal* of the loan. The amount of time for which the loan is made is usually known as the *maturity* or *term* of the loan.

CDs are insured by a government insurance agency called the Federal Deposit Insurance Corporation. The minimum investment balance is usually a few hundred dollars and can be as high as several hundred thousand dollars for some "jumbo" CDs. Needless to say, the interest rates you will receive on CDs are small, but they are usually better than interest rates on regular saving accounts and depend on the level of inflation and the condition of the economy in general. When CDs mature (i.e., the bank has to give you back your principal), you usually have the option of reinvesting in other CDs. Ask your parents about purchasing CDs in the bank they use for their own finances.

U.S. SAVINGS BONDS

Savings bonds are loans American citizens make to the government. There are two types of savings bonds: the Series EE U.S. Savings Bonds (or Series EE Bonds) and the I Savings Bonds. Both types of bonds are low-risk investments that pay interest for up to 30 years. The U.S. Treasury stopped issuing paper savings bonds – you merely register to buy the securities at the website, www.treasurydirect.gov. Like any other investment, you will need your parent or guardian to open up a custodial account in your name if you are a minor.

The way Series EE Bonds work is that you are promised a certain fixed interest rate over a 30-year period. The U.S. Treasury announces the interest rates for new Series EE Bonds each year on May 1 and November 1. At the time of this writing, the interest rate you would earn on a Series EE Bond is a measly 0.10% per year. You have to invest at least $25 in a Series EE Bond, but you cannot invest more than \$10,000 in each calendar year. You can only cash in the bond after one year or more. However, if you cash in the bond before 5 years, you will lose some interest. When you cash in the bond or it matures, you will get the accumulated interest minus penalties for early redemptions, if any.

The I Savings Bonds are similar to the Series EE Bonds with one important distinction: the Series I Bond interest rate is adjusted periodically based on the inflation rate. Specifically, the interest rate is based on a formula, which adds a fixed interest rate, and a rate related to the CPI-U inflation rate. At the time of this writing, the annual interest rate you would earn in the I Savings Bonds is 1.64%.

> For more information, website links, videos, and any assignments associated with this chapter, please visit:
>
> www.teenvestor.com/chapter17

TeenVestor

18

SOCIALLY RESPONSIBLE INVESTING

Just because you have the chance to invest in stocks, mutual funds, and other financial products does not mean that you have to disregard your moral standards. If, for example, your religious upbringing frowns on gambling, you'd probably have to think long and hard before investing in stocks of Las Vegas gaming establishments.

The idea of making investments that meet a set of moral, ethical, or environmental guiding principles is known as socially responsible investing (SRI). Morningstar.com describes why the SRI designation is important in the following paragraph:

> The general premise is to give investors peace of mind by using screens based on moral criteria that create an acceptable universe of investment candidates. Gun manufacturers, distillers, Big Oil, and some pharmaceutical companies typically fail to pass those screens. For example, a religious-themed fund might exclude a pharmaceutical

company that manufactured contraception, even if that product was just one of dozens it produced.

SRI also relates to investing in companies or products that can transform society for the greater good, such as promoting gender equality or a clean and healthy environment.

In recent years, millennials, roughly defined as those born between 1980 and 2000, have been shown in surveys to be more interested in SRI than the generations born earlier. They are concerned about climate change, dependence on fossil fuels, labor practices, and other socially relevant issues. Investment organizations have noticed this trend and are starting to emphasize funds and investments that place a certain portion of investors' money they manage in SRI sectors.

There are various terminologies used to indicate SRI, depending on the emphasis of the investors involved, such as: ESG (economic, social and governance) factor-based investing, sustainable investing, impact investing, values-based investing, community investing, and green investing. To reflect this diversity of terminology, this chapter uses the terms sustainable and responsible investing, sustainable investing, responsible investing, impact investing and SRI interchangeably.

HISTORY OF SOCIALLY RESPONSIBLE INVESTING

SRI has a long history that spans centuries. It was common among religious faiths and indigenous cultures to consider how their economic actions impacted their communities. For example, in the American colonies, Quakers and Methodists abstained from making investments related to the slave trade, war or conspicuous consumption.

In the early stages of SRI, many investors avoided so-called "sin" stocks – stocks of companies involved in producing products or engaged in activities many people dislike for ethical reasons such as alcohol, tobacco, or gambling. In the early 1950s, a mutual fund called the Pioneer Fund became the first to adopt an SRI approach by avoiding investments in any companies involved in the manufacture of tobacco products, alcoholic beverages, or the operation of gambling casinos or other gaming businesses.

Before 1960, most SRI policies involved screening for "sin" stocks. However, the root of sustainable investing since then emerged from the ashes of social movements of the 1960s and 1970s such as the civil rights, feminist, consumer, antiwar and environmental movements. These movements helped highlight often-neglected social, environmental and economic problems and the role corporations and investors can play in resolving them.

The early 1970s also saw the launch of the first modern SRI mutual funds. The Pax World Fund, founded in 1971, and the Dreyfus Third Century Fund, created the next year, were the first funds to combine social and environmental consciousness and financial objectives.

In the 1980s, the anti-apartheid movement, which was opposed to the segregation policies that kept blacks and whites separate in South Africa, picked up steam. By 1993, when South African President Frederik Willem De Klerk took steps to end apartheid, hundreds of companies and institutions had withdrawn their investments in South Africa.

In recent years, a growing number of universities, faith-based institutions, foundations and others have moved to explore their responsibilities in helping to correct "social injuries" caused by companies in which they invested as minority shareholders. The Securities and Exchange Commission (SEC), a regulatory body that oversees the activities of the financial markets, has also made it a bit easier for shareholders to raise questions about environmental and social responsibility at the annual meetings of U.S. publicly traded companies.

Today, we are seeing that social and environmental movements relating to gay rights, immigration, climate change, privacy, and other issues are increasingly becoming part of the conversation about SRI.

CURRENT SRI INITIATIVES

The trend of SRI strategies has led to the establishment of organizations that provide information and services related to sustainability. For example, a research company called Swell Investing is collaborating with Motif Investing (a brokerage firm) to construct investment funds with themes associated with causes such as a) ending cancer, b) upholding human rights, c) fighting poverty, and d) improving education. The fact that these investment models are being created tells you that investors are looking more carefully into the nature of their investments in terms of social responsibility and impact investing.

Further evidence of this trend is that major universities, investment banks and pension funds are setting aside or allocating specific amounts of their money to socially responsible/sustainable investments.

For example, Harvard University's $33 billion endowment (money Harvard uses to fund scholarships and run the university) recently announced that it was signing on to the Principles for Responsible Investment, an initiative supported by the United Nations that relates to SRI.

DO SOCIALLY RESPONSIBLE INVESTMENTS PERFORM?

You may be wondering whether investing in socially responsible companies or funds is as profitable as investing in other companies or funds that don't have any particular mandates to be socially responsible. According to a report issued by the investment bank Morgan Stanley, titled *Sustainable Reality: Understanding the Performance of Sustainable Investment Strategies*, investing in socially responsible companies is more profitable than investing in traditional companies. The link to that report can be found at www.teenvestor.com/chapter18.

HOW TO GAUGE YOUR SRI TOLERANCE

So far, we have defined the meaning of socially responsible investing and the increasing tendency for young people to be interested in making a statement with their investment choices. However, we have not described how to identify companies that are socially responsible. The difficulty in this process is that not everyone may agree on one notion of what is considered socially responsible investing. One person may think gambling is a sin and would avoid any related investments, while another may find it perfectly acceptable to invest in gambling stocks. So socially responsibility is in the eye of the beholder.

Not caring about SRI does not make you a bad person. You may be doing things in your own life to encourage sustainability in your family or your community. For example, you may be involved in your local religious institutions to help the homeless, in recycling programs to reduce waste, and in other activities that reflect your view of what it means to be a good citizen. However, if you choose to extend your general sensibilities about ethics and sustainability to your investments, you need to have some standards in place.

In some cases, it may be easy to see how socially responsible a company is, because its products or mission statements can identify it as socially responsible or not based on a set of moral or ethical principles. For example, some religious investors may classify a tobacco company as not making a sustainable product that lends itself to SRI. Likewise, the stated mission of an ice cream company like Ben & Jerry's has been linked to social responsibility and sustainability from the outset. These two examples are somewhat clear-cut as belonging to one side of the social responsibility spectrum or another.

However, there are some gray areas. A big company that has many divisions may be engaged in some activities that you don't think are socially responsible, but then it may have a charitable arm that encourages green activities. Does that charitable arm make up for the harm that you believe the company is doing in its other divisions? Only you can decide. One way to solve this type of dilemma is to see if the major activity of the company meets your guidelines for socially responsible investing.

As a Teenvestor who may want to invest only in socially responsible stocks or funds, the first thing to recognize is that you cannot solve all of the world's problems at once through your investment decisions. In other words, it is unlikely that you will be able to find companies that meet all of your socially responsible standards. It is best to focus on certain goals such as avoiding companies that manufacture specific products you consider to be dangerous for the world, or investing in companies whose activities are consistent with your views of the general welfare of other human beings. Table 18.1 lists some of the most important SRI considerations used by investment professionals as identified by The Forum for Sustainable and Responsible Investment (US SIF). The table shows the top issues considered by these professionals related to products, social, environmental, and governance (management issues such as executive pay, etc.) concerns. In addition, Column E on the table lists the top combination of SRI considerations used by these investment managers. Keep in mind that some of the items will change based on what is going on in society and the world.

To come up with your own criteria of what makes an SRI, just restrict your considerations to a handful of items. It is easy to avoid certain companies that make products like tobacco and alcohol. But it gets more challenging if, for example, you want to avoid companies that contribute to bad labor practices around the world, because then you would have to know where companies make the components of the products they sell.

Here are some general procedures for how you can screen investments to determine if they are in socially responsible companies or entities:

1. First, determine what is important to you – limit it to 2-4 items from Table 18.1.

2. If you are looking at buying the stock of a company, perform a Google search using the name of the company and "corporate responsibility," "socially responsible investing," or any other term that related to the criteria you have identified.

3. If you are looking at a mutual fund, the prospectus may point you to the fund's stance on socially responsible investing.

4. Visit the company's or mutual fund's investor relations website to see what statements they make about their guidelines associated with your criteria.

TABLE 18.1
Criteria and Concerns Related to Socially Responsible Investing

(A) Top Product Criteria	(B) Top Social Criteria	(C) Top Environmental Concerns
Tobacco	Social – General	Environment – General
Alcohol	Human Rights – Sudan	Climate Change/Carbon
Military/Weapons	General Human Rights	Pollution/Toxics
Gambling	MacBride (Employment principles	Green Building
Pornography	in Northern Ireland)	Clean Technology
Faith-based	Community Relations/Philanthropy	Sustainable Natural
Nuclear	Terrorist or Repressive Regimes	Resources
Products – Other	EEO/Diversity	Environment – Other
Product Safety	Fair Consumer Lending	Fossil Fuel Divestment
Animal Testing/Welfare	Community Services	
Products – General	Affordable Housing	
	Small & Medium Businesses	
	Microenterprise	
	Social – Other	
	Community – General	
	Labor	
	Community – Other	

(D) Top Governance Criteria	(E) Top Combinations (A),(B),(C),(D)
Governance – General	Environment – General
Board Issues	Social – General
Executive Pay	Governance – General
Political Contributions	Tobacco
Governance – Other	Alcohol
	Sudan (To bring pressure to end human rights violations)
	Military/Weapons
	Human Rights
	Gambling
	Climate Change/Carbon
	Pollution/Toxics
	Pornography
	Board Issues
	Faith-based
	Executive Pay (Related to excessive pay of executives)
	Green Building

For more information, website links, videos, and any assignments associated with this chapter, please visit:

www.teenvestor.com/chapter18

19

THE RIGHT TIME AND THE RIGHT WAY TO INVEST

Before you can start investing, you have to accumulate enough money or know that you will be getting money on a regular basis. In addition, you must be able to discipline yourself to invest on a regular basis for a long time. In this chapter, we will discuss when and how to start investing.

WHEN TO START INVESTING

So, you have identified some stocks and mutual funds in which to invest. What do you do next? If you are putting aside a certain amount of money each month in anticipation of investing in stocks or mutual funds, it's a good idea to accumulate at least $50 to $100 each time you want to invest. For mutual funds, you may have no choice anyway, because many of them require that you invest in $100 chunks. For stocks, investing less than $50 is a waste of money, because the investment fees some brokers will charge (as we will discuss later) can be $10 or more each time you buy shares. This will eat into your actual investment amount if you buy stocks frequently. It is probably wise to alert some of your relatives – grandparents, uncles, aunts, and others – to the fact that you invest in chunks of $50 to $100 periodically in stocks and mutual funds, so they can appropriately time and bundle their cash gifts to you.

HOW TO START INVESTING

For people with little money, it is better to choose one or two stocks, invest in them regularly, and hold them for a long, long time. The following sections discuss the process of a periodic investment strategy called *dollar cost averaging.*

Dollar Cost Averaging

You could make lots of money in the stock market if you knew exactly when the price of a stock will hit its low and high points. You simply buy at the low point, and sell at the high point. Sounds easy, right? The truth is that no one can really tell you for sure when prices will move up and down. The only thing anyone can say is that over a very long time, stock prices tend to go up. But even though stock prices go up in the long run, there are periods when the market turns downward. Stock prices, therefore, have their own unpredictable rhythms.

Because predicting the movement of stock prices is virtually impossible, it is best to ignore the market and invest steadily by using the dollar cost averaging approach to investing. With dollar cost averaging, the same amount of money is invested periodically in a stock (or in another financial asset such as a mutual fund), regardless of its price. Some investors use this method because it takes the guesswork out of investing. The technique works because stock prices tend to go up in the long run. The following section, written for the advanced Teenvestor, goes into more details about how dollar cost averaging works.

More on Dollar Cost Averaging (For the Advanced Teenvestor)

The main point about dollar cost averaging is to invest regularly. The investment period could be once a month, once every two months, or any regular time period. Here is how it works.

Suppose you intend to invest $200 every three months to buy as many shares of a company's stock as you can over one year. In that one-year period, you will invest $200 four times, or a total of $800. Suppose also that the prices of a share during the times when you want to make your purchase are as follows: $10, $8, $10, and $12. With this pattern of prices, you will be able to buy the following number of shares (rounded to the nearest whole number):

20 shares calculated as follows: $200 / $10
25 shares calculated as follows: $200 / $8
20 shares calculated as follows: $200 / $10
17 shares calculated as follows: $200 / $12

By the end of the one-year period, you would have purchased a total of 82 shares worth $984 calculated as follows:

82 shares x $12 per share = $984

Now suppose that you hadn't followed the dollar cost averaging technique. If you spent the entire $800 at the beginning of the period, you would have been able to purchase 80 shares (80 = $800/$10). If you spent the entire amount at the end of the period, you would have been able to purchase only about 67 shares ($800/$12). Dollar cost averaging allowed you to purchase 82 shares – more shares than investing the entire amount at the beginning or at the end of the period.

Dollar cost averaging works only when stock prices go up in the long run despite temporary dips. If, for example, the stock prices for the four times you wanted to invest the $200 were $10, $8, $8, and $7, you would have ended up with 99 shares worth $693 ($693 = 99 shares x $7 per share), which is a difference of $107 ($107 = $800 - $693). Still, if you are a long-term investor, you'll stick with this strategy for much more than one year, and chances are you will come out ahead in the end.

WHY DOLLAR COST AVERAGING WORKS

Investing regularly no matter what is happening in the stock market (or with any other financial assets) works because in the long run, stock prices tend to go up. This is in line with our statement earlier in the book that in the past 72 years, the stock market has returned more than 11% per year for investors. To appreciate the importance of investing in a financial asset like a stock over a long time, you have to understand the effect of compounding. We discussed compounding at length in Chapter 10, but it is worth reviewing again.

Compounding is the multiplying effect of investing money in a financial asset over a long time. For example, let's see what happens if you deposit $1,000 in a bank account that pays you 10% interest each year. At the end of the first year, your interest is calculated as follows:

$$\$1,000 \times 10\% = \$100$$

At the end of the first year, the new amount you will have in the bank (if you keep all your money with the bank) will increase by the $100 interest you earned at the end of the year to $1,100. At the end of the second year, you will earn 10% interest again, but this time the interest will be based on the new balance of $1,100 and will be calculated as follows:

$$\$1,100 \times 10\% = \$110$$

At the end of the second year, the new amount you will have in the bank will increase by the $110 interest you earned at the end of the second year to $1,210.

If you keep your money in the bank and earn the interest each year over a long time, the money you have will multiply, because you will be earning interest on top of the interest you earned in previous years. Table 19.1 shows how much an initial deposit of $1,000 in a bank account grows if the interest compounds at 5%, 10%, and 15% annually. Notice how the amount of money in the account grows by leaps and bounds depending on the interest rate. In the 40th year after depositing just $1,000 in the account, the money grows to $11,467 if the interest rate is 5%, $117,391 if the interest rate is 10%, and $1,083,657 if the interest rate is 15%. The compounding effect occurs with any investment, not just a bank deposit, in which you earn a certain return (which is really just like earning interest).

You probably have a hard time even seeing yourself 50 years from now. Just remember that whether it is 5 years, 10 years, 20 years or 50 years, you are better off letting your money grow by keeping it in one place for a long time and letting compounding work for you. In addition, the compounding example we gave above assumed you invested (that is, you put in a bank) $1,000 just one time. Imagine what could happen if you made this investment once a year, year after year, for 50 years. If you invested $1,000 per year for 50 years, you would have $3,566,123 (at 5% per year interest), $13,533,293 (at 10% per year interest) or $63,252,865 (at 15% per year interest) at the end of 50 years. Even if you invest just $1,000 per year for only 10 years, you will have $67,343 (at 5% per year interest), $82,843 (at 10% per year interest) and $102,344 (at 15% per year interest). No matter how you slice it, steady investment over a long time is your best bet to put away money for your future.

TABLE 19.1
A One-Time Investment of $1,000

Yearly Compounding Rates

Years	5%	10%	15%
1	$ 1,050	$ 1,100	$ 1,150
2	$ 1,103	$ 1,210	$ 1,323
3	$ 1,158	$ 1,331	$ 1,521
4	$ 1,216	$ 1,464	$ 1,749
5	$ 1,276	$ 1,611	$ 2,011
6	$ 1,340	$ 1,772	$ 2,313
7	$ 1,407	$ 1,949	$ 2,660
8	$ 1,477	$ 2,144	$ 3,059
9	$ 1,551	$ 2,358	$ 3,518
10	$ 1,629	$ 2,594	$ 4,046
11	$ 1,710	$ 2,853	$ 4,652
12	$ 1,796	$ 3,138	$ 5,350
13	$ 1,886	$ 3,452	$ 6,153
14	$ 1,980	$ 3,797	$ 7,076
15	$ 2,079	$ 4,177	$ 8,137
16	$ 2,183	$ 4,595	$ 9,358
17	$ 2,292	$ 5,054	$ 10,761
18	$ 2,407	$ 5,560	$ 12,375
19	$ 2,527	$ 6,116	$ 14,232
20	$ 2,653	$ 6,727	$ 16,367
21	$ 2,786	$ 7,400	$ 18,822
22	$ 2,925	$ 8,140	$ 21,645
23	$ 3,072	$ 8,954	$ 24,891
24	$ 3,225	$ 9,850	$ 28,625
25	$ 3,386	$ 10,835	$ 32,919
26	$ 3,556	$ 11,918	$ 37,857
27	$ 3,733	$ 13,110	$ 43,535
28	$ 3,920	$ 14,421	$ 50,066
29	$ 4,116	$ 15,863	$ 57,575
30	$ 4,322	$ 17,449	$ 66,212
31	$ 4,538	$ 19,194	$ 76,144
32	$ 4,765	$ 21,114	$ 87,565
33	$ 5,003	$ 23,225	$ 100,700
34	$ 5,253	$ 25,548	$ 115,805
35	$ 5,516	$ 28,102	$ 133,176
36	$ 5,792	$ 30,913	$ 153,152
37	$ 6,081	$ 34,004	$ 176,125
38	$ 6,385	$ 37,404	$ 202,543
39	$ 6,705	$ 41,145	$ 232,925
40	$ 7,040	$ 45,259	$ 267,864
41	$ 7,002	$ 49,785	$ 308,043
42	$ 7,762	$ 54,764	$ 354,250
43	$ 8,150	$ 60,240	$ 407,387
44	$ 8,557	$ 66,264	$ 468,495
45	$ 8,985	$ 72,890	$ 538,769
46	$ 9,434	$ 80,180	$ 619,585
47	$ 9,906	$ 88,197	$ 712,522
48	$ 10,401	$ 97,017	$ 819,401
49	$ 10,921	$ 106,719	$ 942,311
50	**$ 11,467**	**$ 117,391**	**$ 1,083,657**

For more information, website links, videos, and any assignments associated with this chapter, please visit:

www.teenvestor.com/chapter19

20

THE LAW, TAXES AND RECORDS

There are three important aspects of investing that Teenvestors should be aware of: the law regarding young investors, the taxes on investment profits, and the role good record keeping plays in investing.

THE LAW

Minors are not allowed to own stocks, mutual funds, and other financial assets outright. In some states, minors are defined as people younger than 18 years old, and in others they are defined as people younger than 21.

As a minor, you can make investments only under the supervision of your parent through a *custodial account*. One of your parents will have to sign you up for the custodial account. You own the assets in the account, but your parents control the investments in it (hopefully, with your help). According to the law, even though the investments in the account belong to you, you can't sell the investments or do anything on your own as it relates to the account until you are legally an adult. This means that if your state considers you an adult at age 18, you can do whatever you want with the investments in the account at that age.

TAXES

The tax law is quite favorable when it comes to custodial accounts. The Internal Revenue Service (IRS) calls the combination of the following items *unearned income* or *investment income*: interest, dividends and capital gains. The tax laws currently say that if your parents open up a custodial account for you, you can make up to $1,050 of investment income before you have to pay taxes. We have explained all the details to your parents in the next chapter. Read it if you are brave enough, but your parents will probably have to explain some of it to you. Chances are pretty good that you won't have to pay any taxes or fill out any tax forms, because your investments will probably be very small, at least in the beginning.

The math involved in calculating tax is simple. If you have to pay tax on any amount, the tax is determined as follows:

Tax = (Tax Rate) x (Amount Being Taxed)
Where Tax Rate is in percentage terms (such as 15%, etc.)

If you want to know the amount you actually keep after paying taxes, the formula is as follows:

$$\text{After-Tax Amount You Keep} = (1 - \text{Tax Rate}) \times (\text{Amount Being Taxed})$$

Regardless of the current size of your investments, you should keep good records, because your investments may grow to the point where you will have to pay the IRS. In addition, when you keep good records, you will know exactly how much money you are making in specific investments.

RECORD KEEPING

Keeping accurate and up-to-date business records is, for many Teenvestors, the most difficult and uninteresting aspect of investing. Proper record-keeping is important for several reasons. For one thing, the U.S. government wants its share of the money you make by investing in stocks, mutual funds and other investments. It is likely that you won't have to file taxes because you probably won't make that much money on your investments right away. However, a well-designed record-keeping system from the very beginning will help you avoid problems just in case you end up doing really well and have to pay taxes in future years.

In addition, a simple, well-organized system of records, regularly kept up, can actually be a time-saver because it can help you figure out exactly how much money you are truly making on your individual investments. For example, when you buy stocks from an online broker, you should record how much you paid for them as well as the *transaction costs* or *commissions* associated with the purchases. The transaction cost is the commission an online broker charges you to buy or sell an investment. If you don't record your transaction costs, you could end up thinking that you made more money than you actually did. Consider the scenario in the following paragraph.

You buy 4 shares of XYZ stock at the beginning of the year for $30 each, and your online broker charges you $5 to buy the shares and $5 to sell the shares. The amount you give the online broker to buy the shares is $120 before considering the $5 transaction cost associated with the purchase. At the end of the year, the share price for XYZ stock has gone up to $40 per share, so you will receive $160 for the sale of the shares before considering the $5 transaction cost associated with the sale. The simplified before-tax return on investment can be calculated as follows:

Return on Investment = (Ending Value - Beginning Value - Transaction Costs) / Beginning Value

Return on Investment = ($160 - $120 - $5 - $5) / $120 = 0.25 = 25%

Thus, your true return was 25% for the year. If you had not accounted for your transaction costs, which totaled $10, you might have calculated your return as follows:

($160 - $120) / $120 = 0.33 = 33%

By not considering your transaction costs, you would have thought that you made a 33% return on the money you invested instead of the true return of 25%. If you make this kind of mistake, you could end up paying higher taxes than you actually owe.

Another situation where proper record-keeping is important is with capital gains – the profit you make, if any, when you sell a share of stock, mutual funds, and other assets after subtracting your transaction costs. The simplified version of the calculation is as follows:

Capital Gains = (Ending Value - Beginning Value - Transaction Costs)

The calculation in the equation above can be positive or negative. A negative capital gain is another way of saying that you have a *capital loss*; in other words, you lost money on your investment. We won't deal with the case where you have a capital loss here because we hope that when you sell your stocks or mutual funds, you are doing so because you will have positive capital gains.

The amount of tax you owe on your capital gains will depend on how long you have held that stock. The IRS taxes investors less for stocks (and other assets) they hold for over a year than stocks they hold for less than a year. For most Teenvestors, this means that they will be taxed at 15% on the capital gains of a stock (and, for that matter, on any other investment) they sell in less than a year, and 10% on the capital gains of a stock they hold for more than a year. As you can see, to apply these two separate tax rates on capital gains, you have to keep proper records on the price of each stock, the dates on which you bought or sold each stock, the transaction costs or commissions, and so on.

Your record-keeping is made somewhat easier because you will probably not have a big portfolio of investments. Make three copies of Worksheet 20.1 to record your stock, mutual fund, and direct stock purchase transactions.

Worksheet 20.1
Record-Keeping Spreadsheet

Name of Stock/Fund	Date of Purchase or Sale	Number of Shares	Purchase or Sale Price	Commission Paid to Broker, etc.

For more information, website links, videos, and any assignments associated with this chapter, please visit:

www.teenvestor.com/chapter20

21

ONLINE BROKERS

It used to be that you could buy shares of companies only through a handful of companies called *full-service brokers*. These brokers could buy and sell shares for customers, but they charged big fees for each transaction, especially if you bought fewer than 100 shares (or a *round lot* as it is known) of any given stock. For example, you could end up paying up to $100 just to buy 20 shares of a company's stock. These types of brokers claimed that they charged their customers so much for the stock transactions because they provided them with good research information. In truth, customers really had no choice but to use these brokers. Investors either had to invest in stocks through the full-service brokers or keep their money out of the stock market entirely.

Gradually, things began to change. The government made it easier for the existence of *discount brokers* – companies that helped investors buy and sell shares at much lower prices than the full-service brokers (although discount brokers provided very little research on companies). But even though discount brokers slashed the cost of buying and selling shares by half or more, they were still relatively costly, especially for the beginning Teenvestor.

In more recent times, however, the cost of investing has gone down dramatically because of *online brokers* – companies that can sell or buy shares (or mutual funds) for you through the Internet with costs as low as $5 for each transaction. Online brokers such as TradeKing, TD Ameritrade, Capital One Investing, E-Trade, Scottrade, and many others have helped revolutionize the way America buys and sells stock.

The full-service brokers had always boasted that they provided research and advice on companies of interest to investors. Their research and advice was especially helpful for the beginning investor with no clue about which of the thousands of companies out there she should invest in. But even that advantage has gone away, because the Internet is full of free research and financial information that can help investors decide what stocks to buy or sell. And for a small fee, investors can get some of the best research on Wall Street.

While online brokers are plentiful, it can be quite confusing to sift through all the websites to determine which broker best suits your needs. In this chapter, we have drawn up some simple guidelines to help you and your parents decide which broker to use. Just as a reminder, you can't buy and sell stocks unless your parents open a custodial account on your behalf. If you are 18 or older, you can open up your own individual account in most states.

HOW TO CHOOSE A TEENVESTOR-FRIENDLY ONLINE BROKER

One of the first investment decisions you and your parents will have to make, after you decide on companies in which to invest, is what broker to use. Your parents must be involved in this decision, because they will have to fill out the custodial account application you need before you can buy stocks or mutual funds through an online broker. They can also help you understand the pros and cons of going with specific brokers. Here are our suggestions about what to consider when choosing an online broker.

Broker Insurance

Before you can even begin to look at the features offered by an online broker, you should find out whether the broker is insured. The government-sponsored Securities Investor Protection Corporation (SIPC) will cover investments made with reputable brokers. The SIPC insures accounts up to $500,000 against the loss of cash and securities. This insurance covers you if your broker goes bankrupt and has to be liquidated. It doesn't cover you for making poor investment decisions. If a broker is not SIPC insured, you shouldn't invest through that broker under any circumstances.

Minimum Balances

Of course, most Teenvestors are short on cash, so they need online brokers that require little or no minimum balance in a trading account to begin buying stocks. Some of the biggest online brokers that you see being advertised on television (such as E-Trade) require minimum trading account balances of $500 to $2,500. But there are other reputable companies such as TradeKing, TD Ameritrade, and Capital One Investing that have no minimum balance to open trading accounts. You will find though that in some cases, the lower the minimum balance required, the higher the cost per trade, and the higher other trading-related fees.

Low Trading Cost

Trading costs are going down every day. Companies like TradeKing and Capital One Investing are currently charging as little as $4.95 and $6.95 respectively for trading stocks, although trading fees tend to change quickly. Just as some new online-only banks are charging no fees for checking and savings accounts, we see the emergence of no-fee trading accounts as well. One company, Robinhood, is offering a brokerage service to help you buy and sell stocks without paying a dime in commission and without a minimum balance – all through a mobile app. New and economical online brokers are good news for Teenvestors, and we hope (and believe) that trading costs will go down further with all reputable online brokers. However, some of these new companies may not survive because they may find it difficult making a profit without some elements of the traditional business model of the bigger brokers. In Chapter 23, we provide The Teenvestor Ten Online Brokers list which is our current list of Teenvestor-friendly online brokers. This list may change so check our website for updates.

Low Trading Cost
(For the Advanced Teenvestor)

At the time of this writing, you can trade for as low as $5 for what is called a *market order*. This is an order to buy or sell stock at the currently available price. When you place a market order, you can't control the price at which your order will be filled. You simply get the price of the stock at the time the online broker executes your order.

In looking for a good online broker, you may also consider the cost of a *limit order*. This is an order to buy or sell at a specific price. A buy limit order can be filled only at the limit price or lower, and a sell limit order can be filled only at the limit price or higher.

As an example of how a limit order can be better than a market order, suppose that you want to buy the stock of company XYZ that has a current price of $20 per share. You know the price moves around a lot, but you place a market order anyway. If the price jumps to $25 per share, a second after you place your order, the online broker will buy the stock for you at $25 per share and deduct that money from your trading account. In this case, the stock will be purchased for $5 more than the price of $20 when you first placed your order ($25-$20 = $5). The way to protect yourself against this type of price increase is to place a limit order that is slightly above the current price, so you are not forced to buy the stock at a high price if it jumps dramatically. If you had set a limit buy order at $21 per share, the online broker would not have made a purchase until the share price was less than or equal to $21. Thus, the limit order is a ceiling on what you are willing to pay for the stock. Of course, there is a time limit on how long the limit order is open. It can be open for a day or until the price comes down to the limit order.

When you think about it, placing a limit order is not so important if the stock you are thinking about buying does not move around much. Most of the stocks in the Dow, for example, have pretty stable prices compared with some of the technology stocks in the NASDAQ Composite.

Hidden Costs

While a low minimum balance for opening a trading account and a low trading cost are desirable, watch out for hidden costs of other services for which you may be charged. The most common thing for some not-so-reputable brokers to do is to charge low commissions but add handling charges of, say, $5, to the commission. In addition, costs for buying and selling mutual funds may be considerably higher than for buying and selling stocks, so you should consider what type of financial transactions are most likely for you.

All online brokers have a list of their trading prices and service rates on their websites. You should look them over very carefully before deciding which broker to use.

For more information, website links, videos, and any assignments associated with this chapter, please visit:

www.teenvestor.com/chapter21

22

TAXES AND TAX-FRIENDLY INVESTMENTS (For Parents)

The tax issues associated with your Teenvestor's investments center on custodial accounts, IRAs and tuition savings plans. This chapter is not meant as a primer on how to calculate taxes on your Teenvestor's investment portfolio. It is simply a guide to highlight the tax consequences and benefits of the various investment options available to your Teenvestor.

We encourage you to purchase an investment tax guide and visit websites that thoroughly explain investment tax issues before you set up any of the accounts discussed in this chapter. Our website, www.teenvestor.com, will point you to some good tax books and investment websites. If the tax consequences of the custodial accounts, IRAs, and education plans are still not clear after reviewing these investment aids, we urge you to seek the advice of a financial advisor to ensure that there are no adverse tax consequences that would result from your Teenvestor's investment activities.

We must also caution you that as tax rates and tax thresholds change from time to time, some of the figures in this chapter may have changed by the time you read this book. It is very important to check for updates from the IRS or from our website before acting on any of this information.

CUSTODIAL ACCOUNTS

Custodial accounts provide your Teenvestor with a chance to purchase and sell securities under your supervision. These accounts are easy to establish and you can open them for your Teenvestor for stocks, mutual funds, direct stock investment plans, and other assets as long as he has a Social Security number.

A custodial account is held with an adult as the custodian, but in the eyes of the law, the assets in the account belong to the child and are held in his name. The child, however, can't get his hands on the account's assets until he reaches his majority – 18 years old in some states and 21 in others.

The custodian who establishes the account – typically a parent, grandparent or other relative – has management responsibility over the account. In other words, the custodian must be involved in all decisions to buy or sell securities or reinvest earnings generated by the account, even though the investments in the account belong to the minor.

The beauty of establishing a custodial account is that part of the earnings and gains in the account are taxed at a low rate on the average.

Types of Custodial Accounts

There are two types of custodial accounts: the UGMA (named for the Uniform Gifts to Minors Act) and the UTMA (named for the Uniform Transfers to Minors Act). These two types of accounts are very similar in nearly all respects. The most significant difference between the two is the date at which control of the account passes to the child. A custodian loses control over an UGMA account once the child reaches his majority – 18 or 21, depending upon the state. By contrast, a custodian is permitted to postpone transfer of control of an UTMA account to a child, depending upon the state, until 25.

Whether you establish an UTMA or an UGMA account, these accounts have very strict rules that prevent custodians from using them as their personal piggybanks. Furthermore, while you can withdraw money from the account for your child's benefit, the assets in an UGMA account can't be used to pay for things that you are legally obligated to provide to support your child (such as food, clothing, etc.). However, UTMA accounts are more liberal than UGMAs in that they permit funds in the account to be spent for the support of the child.

Disadvantages of a Custodial Account

Criticisms of custodial accounts for children generally fall into three categories. First, even though you may have contributed to the balance in the custodial account to help your child get started as an investor, the assets belong to him. This means that if you wish to close the account and reclaim the assets, you may not only end up paying taxes at your own tax rate on the gains in the portfolio, but you may also find the IRS scrutinizing your actions.

Second, custodial accounts raise thorny issues of "control." Some parents worry that their Teenvestor, upon reaching his majority, will squander the account's assets once he assumes control of the account.

Finally, substantial assets in custodial accounts can reduce a college-bound Teenvestor's eligibility for financial aid or cause tricky estate tax problems if the custodian dies before the child reaches his majority.

Advantages of a Custodial Account

Custodial accounts offer substantial advantages, which we believe outweigh the disadvantages discussed above. The most important advantage of a custodial account is that it enables your Teenvestor to learn how to invest responsibly, early in life, under your supervision. In addition, use of a custodial account will protect more of your Teenvestor's investment income than if he did not have such an account. This is because, as owner of the assets in the account, some of the investment income generated by the account will most likely not be taxed at all, or will be taxed at his rate.

We recommend that you keep the balance in the custodial account modest to minimize concerns such as the adverse tax consequences associated with account closures, loss of custodial control over account assets, reduced financial aid or increased estate taxes.

FILING REQUIREMENTS AND TAX RATES

An in-depth discussion of the tax rules that apply to your Teenvestor's investment activities is certainly beyond the scope of this book. However, it's important that you know about the basic tax rules that govern when an income tax return must be filed for your Teenvestor.

Recognizing When a Tax Return Must Be Filed

As a parent, you should monitor the amount of income that your Teenvestor receives. The IRS defines *investment income* (also known as *unearned income*) as the combination of interest, dividends and capital gains. Investment income should not be confused with *earned income*, which includes salaries, wages, taxable scholarships and grants.

In most instances, your Teenvestor, as a single dependent, will not be required to file or pay taxes on the first $1,050 of investment income (i.e. unearned income). However, once his investment income exceeds $1,050 he must file a tax return or, as discussed below, you may choose to include his investment income on your own tax return.

It is important to recognize that the rules discussed above apply to situations where your Teenvestor's only source of income is investment income. This income will be reported on his tax return, and the amount owed will be calculated on Form 8615, which is to be attached to his return.

Parents can elect to include the investment income of their Teenvestors who are under 19 years of age (or under age 24 if the child is a full-time student) on their own returns. Parents can make this election if their Teenvestor's investment income is more than $1,050 and less than $10,500. If you elect to report this income on your own tax return, your Teenvestor won't have to file a separate return. A parent's tax return that includes the investment income of children must be accompanied by a completed Form 8814.

Gross income is used to determine whether your Teenvestor has to file a tax return when he has *both* investment income and earned income. Gross income, also known as "before-tax" income, is loosely defined as the total of earned income and investment income before any deductions for taxes are taken. Tax returns are required to be filed if your Teenvestor's gross income for the year exceeds the greater of a) $1,050 or b) his earned income plus $350, up to a total of $6,300. Once your Teenvestor's earned income (typically, wages from employment) exceeds $6,300, a tax return must be filed regardless of whether he has any investment income. In addition, if your Teenvestor does not have any investment income and is self-employed – that is, if he is an entrepreneur – he will have to file a tax return if his net profit exceeds $400.

Determining the Appropriate Tax Bracket

Obviously, understanding when your Teenvestor is required to file a tax return is just one piece of the puzzle. It is also important to understand how to figure the tax rate that will be applied to his investment income.

Your Teenvestor is required to pay taxes on investment income exceeding $1,050. The tax rate that will apply to this income depends upon whether your Teenvestor is younger than 19 or not. If he is under 19 and has investment income, he is subject to the *kiddie tax*. Technically speaking, the kiddie tax is not actually a tax but rather a restriction that seeks to prevent parents from transferring their investment assets to their children under 19 to shield their income from taxes.

Under the kiddie tax, investment income over $1,050 and up to $2,100 will be taxed at your Teenvestor's tax rate. For most Teenvestors, this should probably be 10%. Any investment income over $2,100 will be taxed at the parent's tax rate.

INDIVIDUAL RETIREMENT ACCOUNTS (IRAs)

Another investment option available to Teenvestors is an Individual Retirement Account, or IRA. IRAs are tax-advantaged accounts that can be set up for retirement or educational purposes. They have a different set of restrictions from custodial accounts. In the sections below, we consider three different types of IRAs: the Roth IRA, the traditional IRA, and the Educational IRA.

Socking money away for the "big payoff" at retirement five decades down the road is not going to motivate the average Teenvestor to invest in an IRA. Your Teenvestor will need a little incentive from you to get going with an IRA, even though you may think the only incentive he needs is that it's for his own good.

We'd like to suggest that you make the initial deposit in your Teenvestor's IRA account to get him started. You can also try a savings matching incentive program whereby you contribute more to an allowance, for example, if he conscientiously contributes money to the IRA from time to time. Do anything, including impounding a portion of cash gifts from relatives, to strongly encourage him to make contributions to an IRA, especially if he has no other investments.

Your Teenvestor may find it easier to maintain an IRA if he knows that one particular type of IRA, the Roth IRA, allows early withdrawals of contributions without a tax penalty as described in more detail below.

Roth IRAs

The *Roth IRA* has been increasingly popular since its enactment into law in 1997. An investor can make annual contributions with after-tax dollars to a Roth IRA account and accumulate earnings until age 59½, at which time he can withdraw the money tax-free. Your Teenvestor can establish a Roth IRA and buy stocks, bonds, and other assets for the account just like for a regular, non-IRA custodial account.

Original *contributions* to a Roth IRA, as opposed to accumulated earnings (loosely coined, the profits generated by the account), can be withdrawn tax-free *prior* to age 59½ without a penalty, after five years. If, however, your Teenvestor withdraws all his contributions, then proceeds to withdraw the accumulated earnings in the portfolio before turning 59½, he will not only pay taxes on the earnings but will also pay a 10% penalty. There are limited exceptions to this rule, including withdrawals for paying qualified education expenses. You will find more details in our website, www.teenvestor.com/chapter22.

A Roth IRA, like any other IRA, can be set up through a bank or stockbroker. Many brokerage firms will open custodial IRAs for children. However, fees and minimum balances vary, so it is necessary to shop around. To qualify as a Roth IRA, the account must be specifically designated as such. Contributions to the account must be made in the form of money (cash, check or money order), and that money can then be used to buy stocks, mutual funds, and other assets for the account.

While a Teenvestor can have more than one type of IRA in addition to the Roth IRA, such as a traditional IRA and a Coverdell Educational Savings Account (described below), his combined contributions to a Roth and traditional IRA can't exceed the lesser of his total yearly wages or $5,500. This means that if your Teenvestor's taxable compensation is less than $5,500, he may only contribute as much as he earns. If he earns more than $5,500 per year, the maximum he can contribute each year is $5,500. Teenvestors can't contribute to their IRA in years in which they have no earned income. On the other hand, once the IRA is established, it is not necessary to contribute to it for every year in which income is earned. Account holders are not permitted to contribute more than the amount allowable for the year to "make-up" for years in which little or no contribution was made.

Anyone who works and thus receives earned income, or more specifically, taxable compensation (defined to include wages, salaries, tips, and amounts received for providing personal services), during the year can establish a Roth IRA.

Both Roth and traditional IRAs (discussed below) have income limitations, which restrict higher wage earners from investing in them. It's unlikely that your Teenvestor needs to be concerned with these limitations, because his earned income would probably not reach the income limitations. However, if you are concerned that your Teenvestor may be subject to these thresholds, we recommend that you consult IRS Publication 590-A (*Contributions to Individual Retirement Arrangements*) and a tax or investment consultant for more information.

Traditional IRAs

A *traditional IRA* allows your Teenvestor to make annual tax-deductible contributions. The contributions to the account are tax deferred until he reaches age 59½, at which point he can withdraw the money and get taxed at his tax rate at the time of the withdrawal. His tax rate at age 59½ or later will probably be much lower than his tax rate during his working years. Your Teenvestor can buy stocks, bonds, and other assets with the money in the account just like a regular non-IRA custodial account or a Roth IRA.

As with Roth IRAs, your Teenvestor may only invest in a traditional IRA if he has earned income. This means the traditional IRA raises the same "earned income" questions as discussed in the previous section concerning Roth IRAs. Traditional IRAs are also subject to the same contribution thresholds as Roth IRAs (namely, taxable compensation up to $5,500 per year), and are set up the same way as Roth IRAs.

There are two significant drawbacks to traditional IRAs. First, upon retirement, withdrawals from the IRA are taxed. As discussed above, with a Roth IRA, once the investor has reached age 59½, withdrawals from the account are tax-free. Second, contributions to traditional IRAs can't be withdrawn before age 59½ without a 10% penalty in addition to the payment of regular income taxes. There are a limited number of exceptions to this rule, including withdrawals for paying qualified education expenses. By contrast, the Roth IRA permits withdrawal of original contributions prior to 59½ for any reason (after five years). For these reasons, many investment experts believe the Roth IRA is superior to a traditional IRA, especially for young people with very little or no earned income.

Coverdell Educational Savings Account

You can also help your Teenvestor open up a Coverdell Educational Savings Account (ESA), a type of account established by Congress exclusively for the purpose of tax-deferred saving for higher education expenses. Qualifying higher education expenses include tuition, fees, books, supplies, equipment, and in the event that the Teenvestor is at least a half-time student, room and board. ESAs must be so designated when they are established. While your Teenvestor may have more than one ESA, the total of all contributions to all ESAs can't exceed $2,000 per tax year. Parents, grandparents, other relatives, friends, and your Teenvestor for whom the account is being established can contribute to an ESA.

ESAs are similar to Roth IRAs in several ways. First, contributions to an ESA are not tax deductible. However, withdrawals are tax-free for payment of qualifying higher education expenses. Second, ESAs are subject to the same income limitations as Roth IRAs. Third, early withdrawals from ESAs are subject to the same 10% penalty rule for early withdrawals as traditional IRAs and Roth IRAs.

Unlike traditional IRAs and Roth IRAs, your Teenvestor can invest in an ESA whether or not he is employed. Contributions to an ESA do not have to be combined with contributions to a traditional IRA or a Roth IRA. This means that your Teenvestor can invest $2,000 in an ESA while simultaneously contributing a combined maximum of $5,500 in a traditional IRA and a Roth IRA.

College Tuition Savings Plans

The primary drawback to the ESA is its $2,000 maximum annual contribution amount. By contrast, college tuition savings plans (also known as 529 Plans), with their higher contribution maximums, are considered to be good investment vehicles to help parents and Teenvestors plan for college education. Under these plans, money is invested in a state-sponsored fund designed to help save for college tuition (and associated expenses such as room, board, books, and supplies). Most plans are open to both state residents and non-residents, and the assets in the funds can be used to pay for education expenses at virtually any college in the country.

Earnings in college tuition savings plans are not subject to federal tax, and in most cases, state taxes, as long as you use withdrawals for eligible college expenses, such as tuition and room and board. You will find links to each state's college tuition plans on our website at www.teenvestor.com/chapter22.

MISCELLANEOUS TAX ISSUES ASSOCIATED WITH THE TYPICAL INVESTOR

At some point, many Teenvestors will receive cash or stock dividends or sell assets in their portfolios. In the event that your Teenvestor receives a dividend or sells assets in his account, a general understanding of the tax implications of the transaction would be helpful. For this reason, we include in this section a brief discussion of the basic tax rules applicable to cash dividends, stock dividends, capital gains and capital losses.

Cash or Stock Dividends

Corporations may elect to pay ordinary dividends to their shareholders, which are paid out of the earnings and profits of a corporation. While corporations can pay other types of dividends, you can assume that any type of dividend that your Teenvestor receives on common or preferred stock is an ordinary dividend unless the paying corporation tells you otherwise. These dividends will be shown in box 1 of the Form 1099-DIV that you receive.

As we discussed in an earlier section, if your Teenvestor receives cash dividends, these dividends are treated as investment income. But what if he receives stock dividends? The general rule for stock dividends is that if your Teenvestor had no choice as to whether to receive either a cash or stock dividend, no income tax will be due on the stock dividend until the stock is sold. However, if he elected to receive the stock dividend, it is treated in the same manner as receipt of cash dividends; it's added to his investment income in accordance with the tax-paying rules described earlier in this chapter.

Consideration of the tax rules applicable to mutual funds and Dividend Reinvestment Plans (DRIPs) is beyond the scope of this chapter. We recommend that you consult a good tax book or an accountant to sort out these issues. For those up to the task, IRS Publication 550 (*Investment Income and Expenses*) and Publication 564 (*Mutual Fund Distributions*), as well as the relevant section of the 1099-DIV form (*Capital Gains Distributions on 1099-DIV Forms*) are helpful resource guides.

Capital Gains and Losses

Throughout this book, we have stressed the importance of Teenvestors holding assets in their portfolio for the long term. Our basic goal has been to show Teenvestors how to make prudent and responsible investments. There may come a time, however, when your Teenvestor finds it necessary to sell assets in his portfolio. His profits (*capital gains*) or losses (*capital losses*) will have to be accounted for from a tax standpoint and reported on Schedule D (Form 1040). While the discussion below addresses capital gains and losses on stocks, we note that these concepts are generally applicable to mutual funds, bonds, and other assets.

The amount of tax owed on capital gains depends on the cost basis of the stock or other assets, how long the seller held the asset, and his income level. In order to determine the *cost basis* of stock, for example, it is necessary to know how the seller acquired the stock. If the

Teenvestor purchased the stock through a custodial account, the cost basis is the purchase price plus commissions. If the stock is inherited, the cost basis is the fair market value of the stock at the date of the individual's death. If the stock was a gift, calculating the cost basis gets a little trickier. For our purposes, we need only note that in general, the cost basis of stock given as a gift is the donor's cost basis and, if the donor had to pay a gift tax, this is included as well. In addition, there are several ways to calculate the cost basis of mutual funds. We recommend that you consult a tax guide for more information in this area since the determination of taxes can be quite involved. Fortunately, your Teenvestor will most likely not make so much money as trigger any tax obligations.

For more information, website links, videos, and any assignments associated with this chapter, please visit:

www.teenvestor.com/chapter22

TeenVestor

23

THE TEENVESTOR TEN

This chapter reveals the results of our analysis of the various investment, information, and banking websites available on the Internet. Admittedly, personal judgment comes into play here, but we also had some young people look at the websites to see whether they could get the information they sought on stocks, mutual funds, and bank accounts. Our lists were compiled based on the opinions of these young people and on our own feelings as to the usefulness of the information provided by the websites. The best websites are dubbed the The Teenvestor Ten for banking, education, research, current business news, and online brokers.

Features offered by financial websites and institutions change. In addition, new websites that provide better information can show up overnight and companies that offer financial services can merge with other institutions. For these reasons, The Teenvestor Ten lists will change from time to time. Please check our website for adjustments to our lists. As a first step in choosing Teenvestor-friendly information websites and services, we eliminated those that charge Teenvestors for accessing information. In addition, we eliminated websites that required too much personal information of the user (unless you are subscribing to banking services), and websites that were too difficult to use or were simply too cluttered.

On our website, www.teenvestor.com/chapter23, you will find links to the companies that made The Teenvestor Ten list in each of the five categories.

BANKING

Your "savings" are usually put into the safest places or products that allow you access to your money at any time. Examples include savings accounts, checking accounts, and certificates of deposit. Whether you are selecting a traditional bank or an online bank that has no physical offices, it's wise to make sure that it is legitimate and that your deposits are federally insured by the Federal Deposit Insurance Corporation (FDIC). The FDIC is an independent agency of the United States government that protects you against the loss of your deposits if an FDIC-insured bank or savings association fails. FDIC insurance is backed by the full faith and credit of the United States government. Since the FDIC's creation in 1933, no depositor has ever lost even one penny of FDIC-insured deposits.

The Internet is a public network. Therefore, it is important to learn how to safeguard your banking information, credit card numbers, Social Security Number and other personal data. Look at your bank's website for information about its security practices, or contact the bank directly. One of the most important security features regarding online banking is encryption.

Encryption is the process of scrambling private information to prevent unauthorized access. To show that your transmission is encrypted, some browsers display a small icon on your screen that looks like a lock or a key whenever you conduct secure transactions online. Avoid sending sensitive information, such as account numbers, through unsecured e-mail.

In choosing the banks on this list, we considered whether they had a mobile app, whether they charge little or no fees associated with their checking accounts, and whether they require little or no minimum balances to open accounts. We were not very concerned about the interest rates they pay on account balances but you can easily get that information on your own.

You should be aware, however, that you may not get the same full service from online-only banks as you would from traditional banks such as Bank of America or J.P. Morgan Chase. For example, you may not get live operator 24/7 support with online-only banks although you may be able to get a live chat. In addition, online-only banks may not have the same number of ATMs for easy access to your money. However, if your banking needs are simple, this may not matter to you. Most Teenvestors we know just don't want their small amount of savings whittled away by maintenance fees and they don't like being severely dinged for inadvertent overdrafts.

The Teenvestor Ten (for Banking)

BankMobile	www.bankmobile.com
Simple	www.simple.com
Moven	www.moven.com
CapitalOne360	www.capitalone360.com
Ally Bank	www.allybank.com
First Internet Bank	www.firstib.com
Bank5 Connect	www.bank5connect.com
Key Bank	www.keybank.com
iGoBanking	www.iGoBanking.com
GoBank	www.gobank.com

EDUCATION

Before a Teenvestor even begins to buy stocks or mutual funds, she must understand basic investing principles. This book is a start, but there are lots of educational materials available on the Internet. Most of them will do for your purposes. However, we first looked around for substantive websites that were specifically written for Teenvestors. Then we moved on to websites for beginning investors.

Needless to say, we think our website, www.teenvestor.com, is the most comprehensive teen investment education website there is. Our website also gives numerous links to other websites to help you along the way and lists organizations that can help young people learn more about investing. All in all, www.teenvestor.com should be your first stop when you begin your investment journey. Here are The Teenvestor Ten Educational Websites:

The Teenvestor Ten (for Education)

Teenvestor	www.teenvestor.com
Investopedia	www.investopedia.com
The Motley Fool	www.fool.com
InvestorGuide	www.investorguide.com
The Vanguard Group	www.vanguard.com
E-Trade	www.etrade.com
TD Ameritrade	www.tdameritrade.com
Securities and Exchange Commission	www.sec.gov
Morningstar	www.morningstar.com
Capital One Investing	www.capitaloneinvesting.com

RESEARCH

A Teenvestor must do her own research before investing in any stocks or mutual funds. This research need not be difficult if she goes to the right websites. We found that some research websites were too difficult to use. To be sure, most of them provide the same types of information, but some were better organized than others. In addition, we found that too many websites assumed an advanced knowledge of the market.

Although we feel that a Teenvestor can muddle through any research website and eventually get the information she needs, we decided to include on our list the best-organized websites and those that beginning investors can truly use with ease. Some of the criteria we used in determining our top research websites included availability of the following information: stock quotes (historical graphs are a plus), company descriptions, industry comparisons, earnings data (historical PE ratios, EPS, ROE, etc.), earnings growth rates, market capitalizations, balance sheets, and other financial information. Here are The Teenvestor Ten Research Websites:

The Teenvestor Ten (for Research)

Yahoo!Finance	www.finance.yahoo.com
Marketwatch	www.marketwatch.com
Morningstar	www.morningstar.com
Securities and Exchange Commission	www.sec.gov
MSN Money	www.msn.com
InvestorGuide	www.investorguide.com
The Street	www.thestreet.com
Bloomberg	www.bloomberg.com
Scottrade	www.scottrade.com
Zacks Investment Research	www.zacks.com

CURRENT NEWS ABOUT COMPANIES

The research websites in the previous section often have recent articles about public companies. But we find that it is sometimes better to go to websites that specialize in gathering news on a daily basis for up-to-date information on these companies. Here are The Teenvestor Ten Current Business News Websites:

The Teenvestor Ten (for Current Business News)

Market Watch	www.marketwatch.com
CNBC	www.cnbc.com
CNN Money	www.money.cnn.com
The Street	www.thestreet.com
Yahoo!Finance	www.yahoo.com
New York Times	www.nytimes.com
Bloomberg	www.bloomberg.com
MSN Money	www.msn.com
Business Insider	www.businessinsider.com
Washington Post	www.washingtonpost.com

ONLINE BROKERS

Online brokers offer investors a lot on their websites to entice them to sign up. They even add a lot of educational and research material just to get you to become informed enough about the stock market so that you are comfortable buying shares through them. However, we take a simplified approach to online brokers because we don't really care about all the "bells and whistles" they offer to investors. We just want to know whether Teenvestors can primarily buy stocks cheaply through them (using custodial accounts) without holding big cash balances in their investment accounts. All other considerations, such as getting "real-time" stock quotes as opposed to stock prices delayed by 15 minutes, should be of no real concern to the Teenvestor who just wants to invest whatever little money she has in the stock market for a long period of time. Here now are The Teenvestor Ten Online Brokers:

The Teenvestor Ten (for Online Brokers)

TradeKing	www.tradeking.com
Robinhood	www.robinhood.com
Kapitall	www.kapitall.com
OptionsHouse	www.optionshouse.com
OptionsXpress	www.optionsexpress.com
Capital One Investing	www.capitaloneinvesting.com
TD Ameritrade	www.tdameritrade.com
Fidelity	www.fidelity.com
E-Trade	www.etrade.com
Scottrade	www.scottrade.com

For more information, website links, and videos associated with this chapter, please visit:

www.teenvestor.com/chapter23

TeenVestor

INDEX